How to Draw Portraits and Caricatures of

BABIES

Coloring and Tracing Workbook

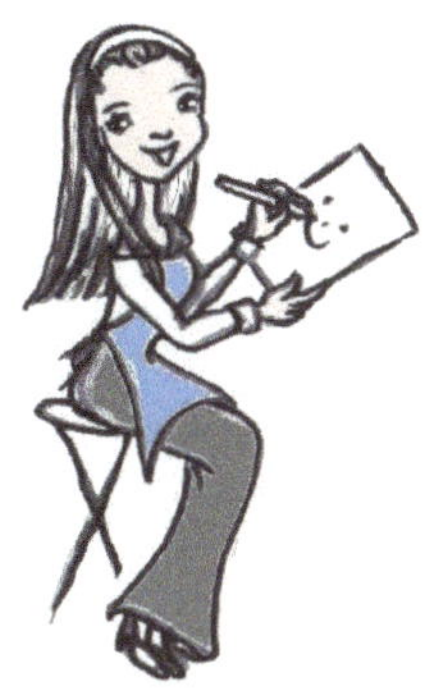

By Artist Marta Sytniewski

This book is dedicated to my children

Natalia, Axel and Liliana

to enkindle in them joy in studying
portraiture and love for children—
masterpieces of God's Love

Introduction

This book can be enjoyed as a relaxing pastime and as a learning tool for people of all ages and skill levels. It encourages learning through observation, imitation, and practice while providing opportunities to color, trace, and draw creatively. A valuable asset and a great resource for any art class, this book unveils the world of professional portraiture and caricature art through the eyes of a working artist. Charming examples of the use of line weight, the rendering of light and shadow, and the creation of flesh tones can be found throughout the artist's original artworks. While using this book, you may develop muscle memory for coloring, tracing, and drawing, and develop visual memory for portraiture and caricature art depicting babies. For some people, creating and observing art that depicts happy babies can generate emotional and psychological benefits, and I hope this book leads you to them.

☑ **Develop muscle memory.** Practice coloring, tracing, and drawing in a full-page format directly in this book. Creating artworks of similar subjects, such as children, may facilitate muscles to consolidate this task into motor memory. In time, your muscles might take over and free up your concentration so that you can genuinely enjoy the artistic process. Muscle memory for coloring and drawing may make your art **more enjoyable** as you complete it **faster** and with **less conscious effort**.

☑ *Develop visual memory.* Many people are visual learners, for this reason, this book contains original portrait and caricature drawings in addition to the coloring and tracing pages. By studying and creating artwork, you may begin to develop visual memory—an intuitive sense of baby portraiture. Familiarize yourself with a wealth of different baby facial features, structures, and expressions. Learning from observation, over time, may help you draw babies from memory and in real-life settings as well as expand your skill to other fields, such as cartoon and illustration.

☑ *Experience psychological and emotional benefits.* Coloring and looking at art of happy babies, such as the ones in this book, may facilitate emotional and psychological benefits. Enjoy the coloring and tracing process. Coloring and viewing art may help you fall into a contemplative state of flow, releasing endorphins and providing you with positive, purposeful engagement and a sense of accomplishment. There is also spiritual and educational value that may be gained from engaging in this book. Children—with their innocence, trust, and love—lead us closer to God. It is easy to feel happy doing something as precious as coloring, tracing, drawing, and enjoying this book. I truly hope you enjoy *How to Draw Portraits and Caricatures of Babies: Coloring and Tracing Workbook.*

Share the Love

Draw for others. Portrait and caricature art, brings happiness to the people you draw—your subjects. Art can be a thoughtful and personal gift for loved ones, strangers, and even for special occasions like birthdays.

Fundraise. Share the love of art through fundraising. You can:

- ☑ donate art that you have made,
- ☑ draw something specific for the people and organizations you are helping
- ☑ provide live caricature entertainment to raise funds for a charitable cause, or
- ☑ teach others to draw through workshops, classes, tutorials, and through sharing this book.

This book will provide you with plenty of practice in drawing portraits and   caricatures. I wish I had such a practical resource and learning tool as this book when I began drawing, therefore I developed this workbook so that my children and students will have an easy and enjoyable start in their portrait and caricature careers. I started drawing caricatures to entertain guests and raise funds for the Home of Single Mothers charity events.

Later, I drew caricatures to fundraise at local churches, catholic schools, and charity banquets. I also drew caricatures and portraits as gifts for family and friends.

Use your skills and talent to bring joy to the people you love and help the churches and charity organizations in your area. <u>You will be a blessing to others, you will receive blessings a thousandfold, and you will accumulate treasures in Heaven.</u>

Help people in the long term.

Do you know someone who likes drawing or needs a career? Do you know someone who needs something positive in their life? This: *How to Draw Portraits and Caricatures of Babies: Coloring and Tracing Workbook* may be what they need to feel better or to overcome a difficult time in their life.

This unique, *learn from coloring, tracing, drawing, and observation* book is a fun and valuable resource to engage people of any age or skill level. Share the joy of coloring and experiencing art! Purchase this book as a gift for those who could use a little positivity and beauty in their lives.

May God bless you and lead you in your creative goals.

Materials

Dry media, such as colored pencils, pastel pencils, charcoal, and graphite are best suited for coloring inside this book. I completed all the finished artwork in this book using fine art soft pastels, but please feel free to use any dry media you desire.

Wet media drawing and coloring supplies, including markers and watercolors, are not recommended for use inside the book, because the ink can bleed through the paper onto the other side. To minimize bleed-through effects, this book is printed on high-quality paper that is especially suited for drawing. Additionally, the coloring and tracing pages are mirror representations of each other.

Pages in this book can also be taken out at your convenience to study both the coloring pages and the finished artworks simultaneously. Book pages can also be taken out for framing and display purposes.

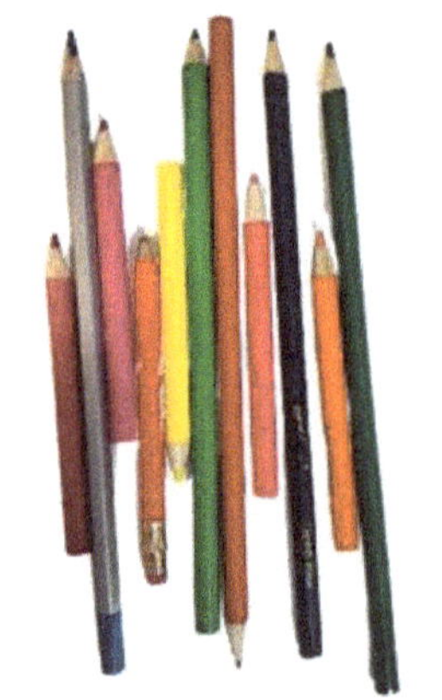

Pastel Pencils

Colored Pencils

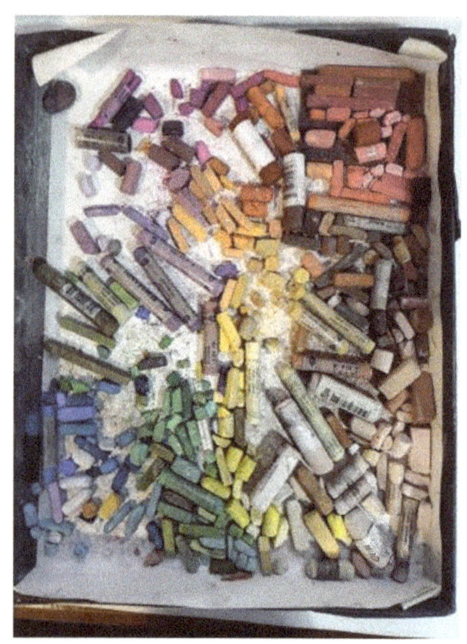

Soft Pastels

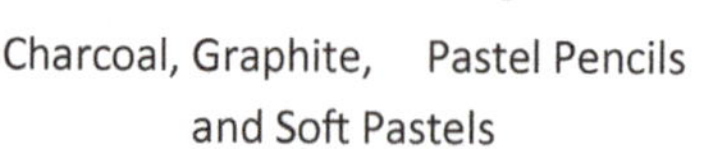

Charcoal, Graphite,   Pastel Pencils
and Soft Pastels

Color

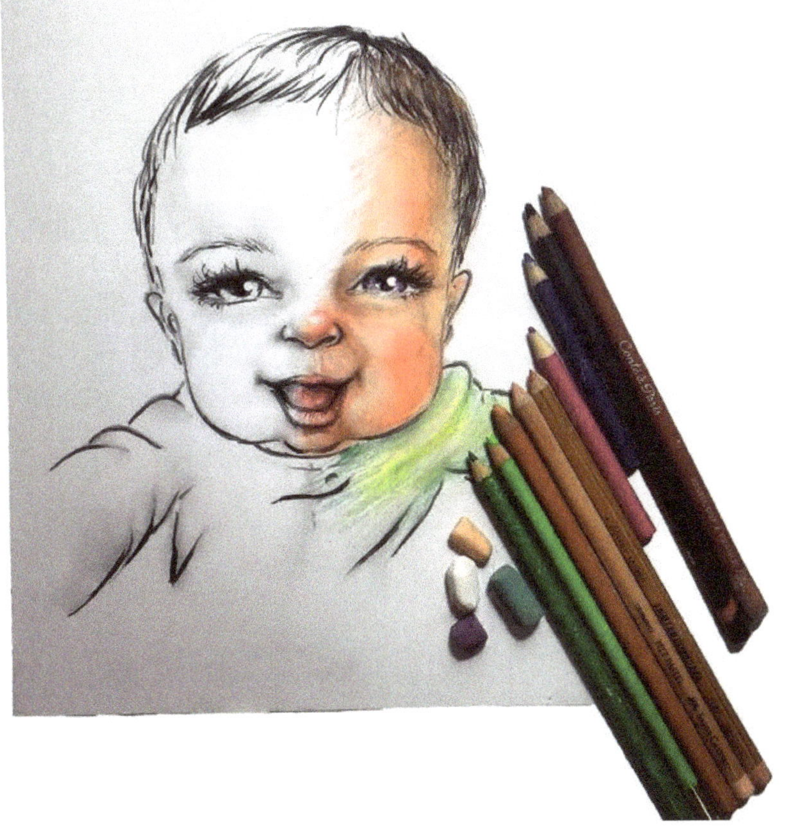

Study Original Artworks

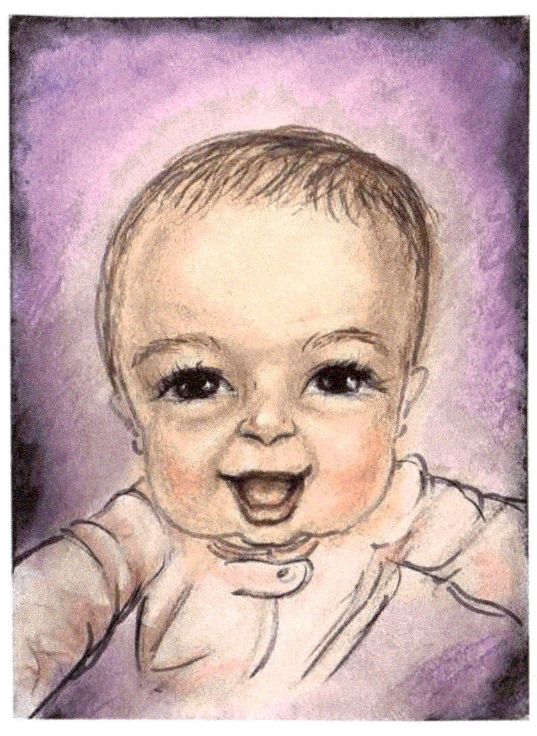

Trace

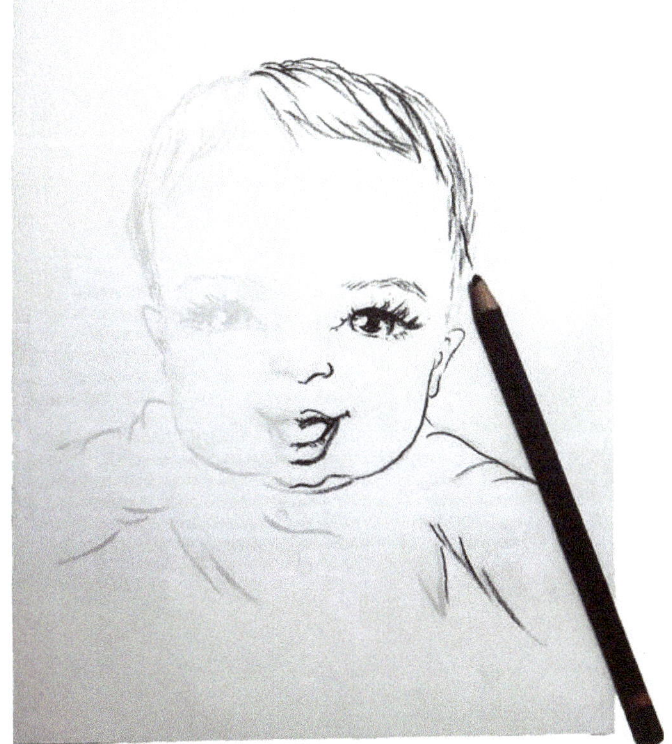

Draw Independently

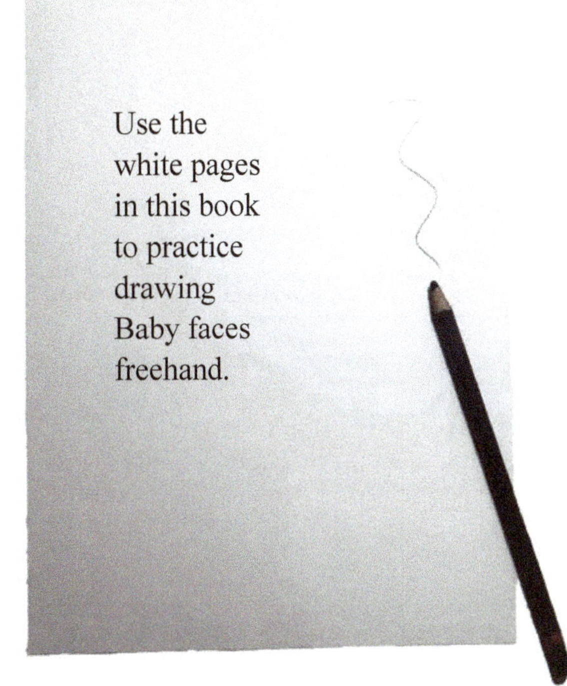

Use the
white pages
in this book
to practice
drawing
Baby faces
freehand.

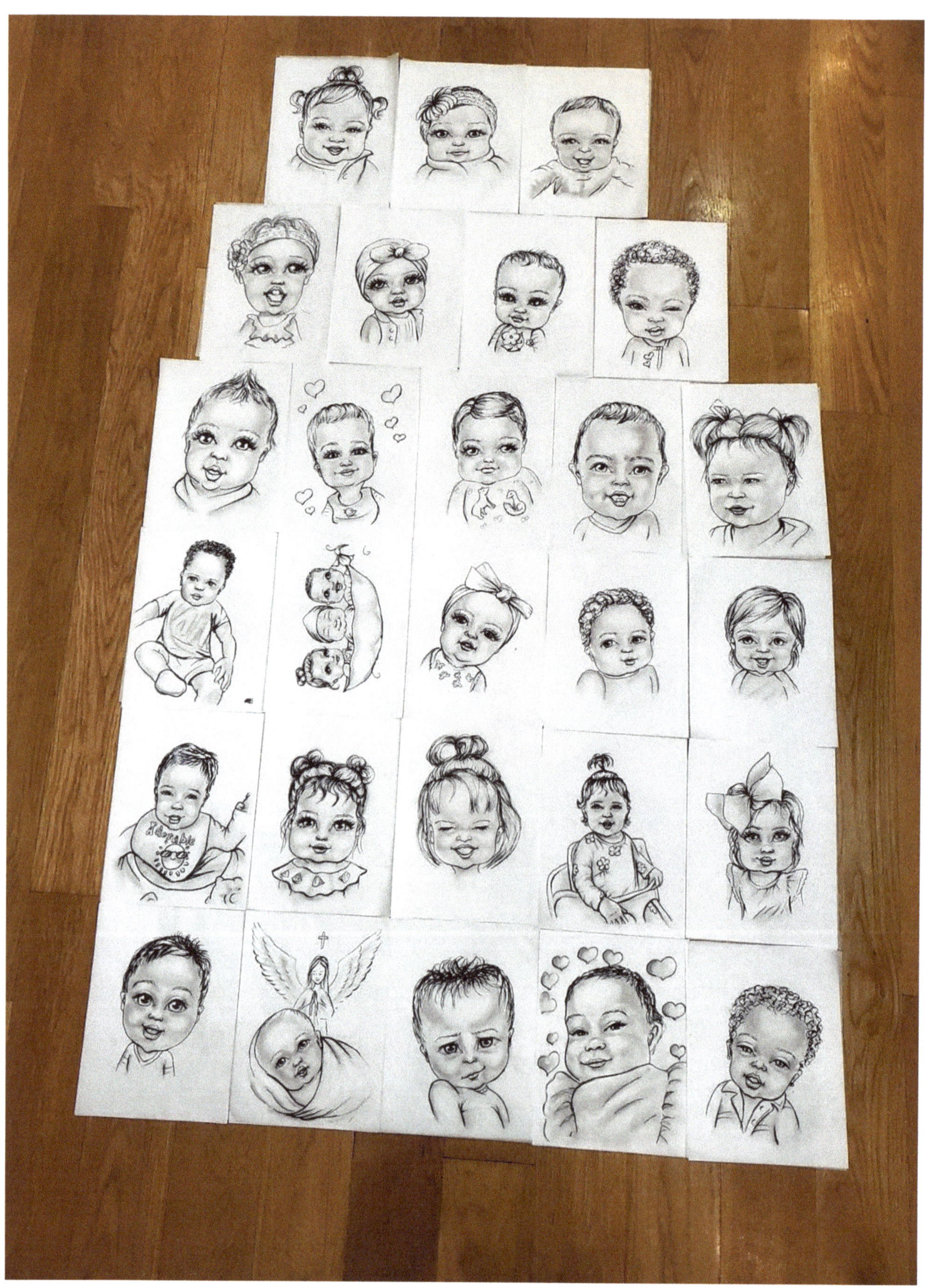

Artist Marta Sytniewski * www.FunnyAndCuteCaricatures.com * FunnyAndCuteCaricatures

Coloring Page Creation Process

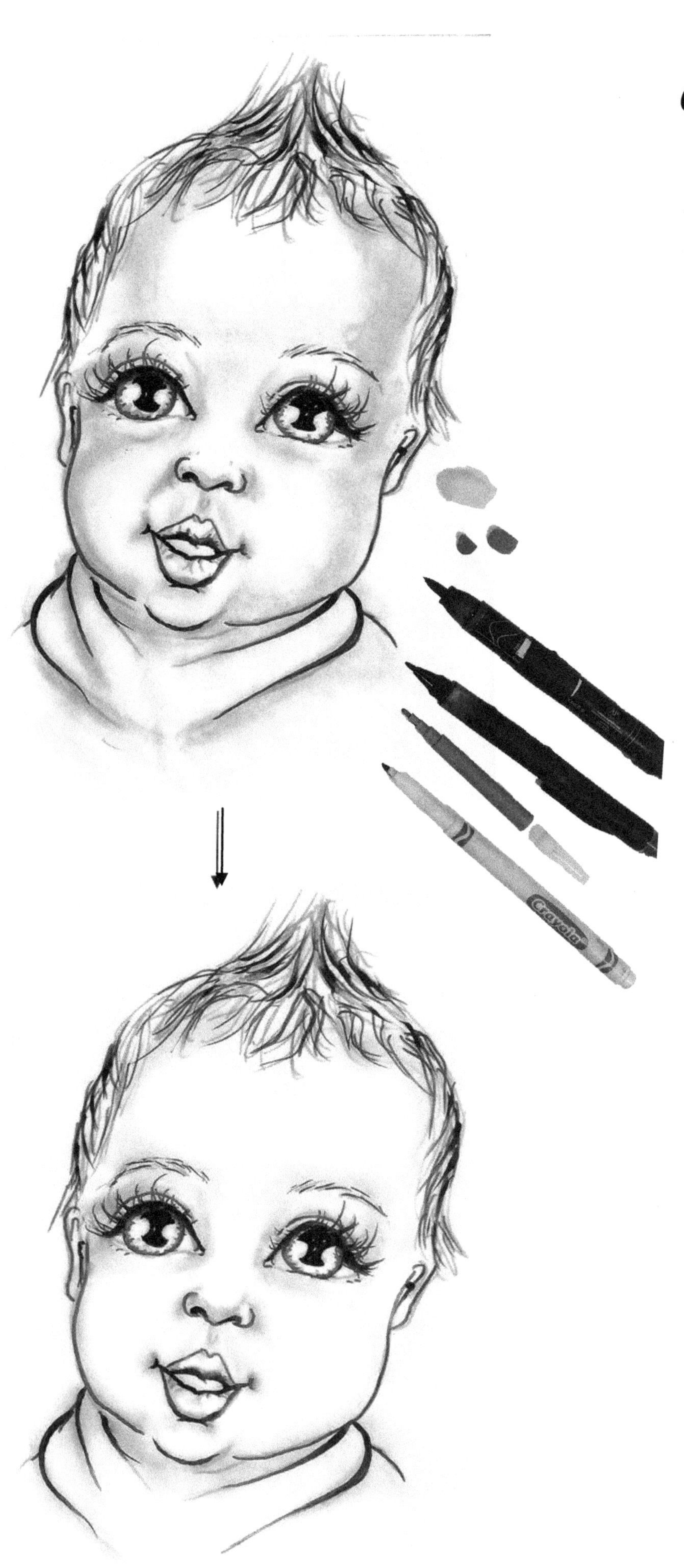

I completed the colored artworks in this book live in my art gallery during my career as a professional portrait and caricature artist. I modeled the coloring pages after my original portraits and caricatures.

I used a variety of gray and black markers to create the coloring pages, giving the artworks a rich variation of line density and depth that is well-suited for coloring and tracing. *The* drawings were then lightly shaded in gray and white, using soft pastels, in traditional drawing methods. Subsequently, the coloring pages were scanned into the computer and the pastel shading was manually softened using computer software.

Grayscale coloring pages make it easy for students to accomplish more realistic, three-dimensional effects with less effort, because some of the rendering has already been done. A more three-dimensional result can provide a deeper sense of satisfaction and accomplishment.

When working with grayscale coloring pages, you may become more familiar with the effects of lights and shadows. Practice makes perfect, and this book offers three ways to practice through coloring, tracing, and drawing independently. Utilize observation, comparison, and contrast of your work to the original finished artworks in this book. Use your creativity, color the drawing pages in different colors, or monochrome. Have fun while gaining experience in baby portrait and caricature art.

Practice makes perfect. By coloring, tracing, and drawing similar subjects multiple times, you may develop visual and muscle memory.

You may also gain experience and confidence as an artist.

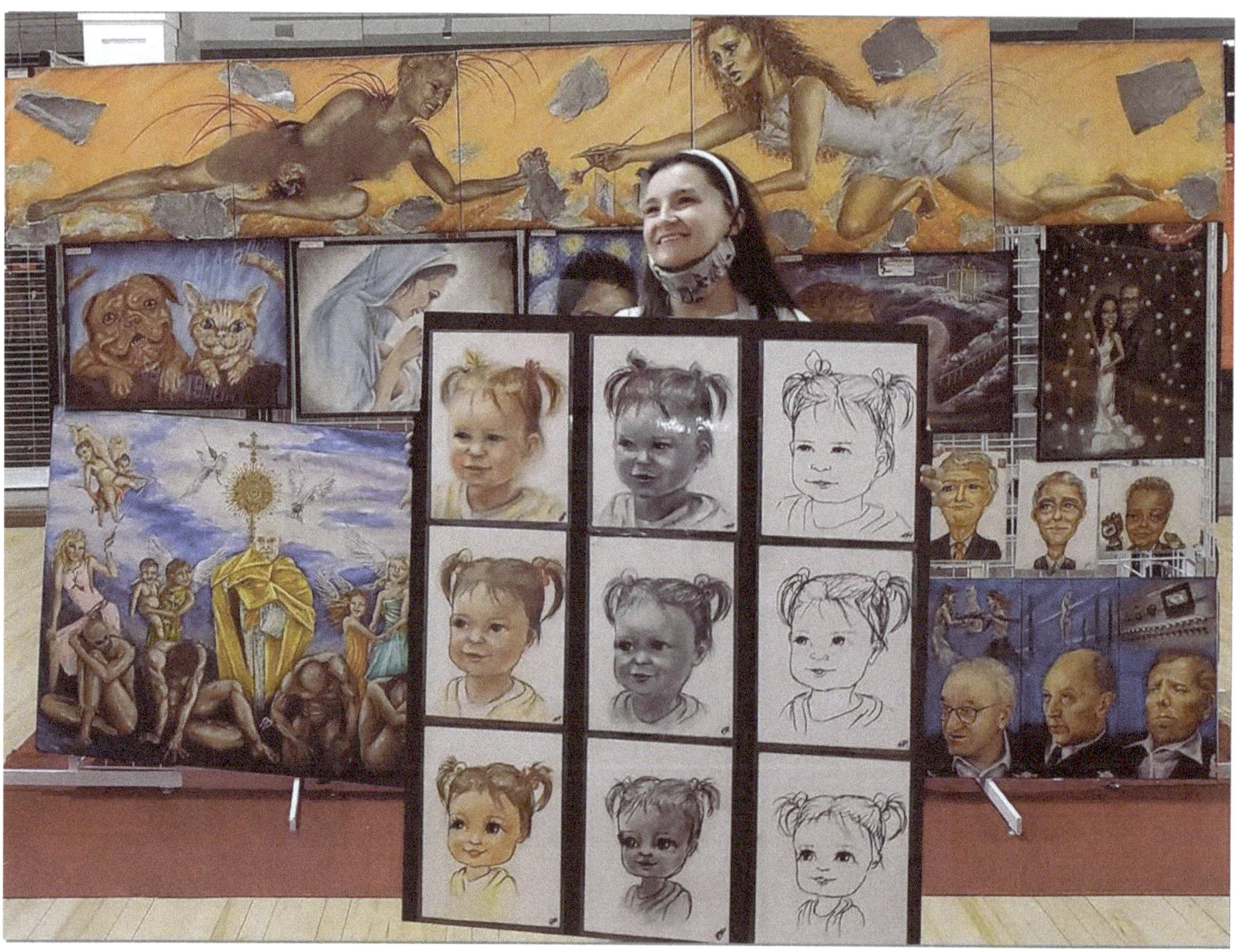

Here I drew my daughter Liliana in nine different styles.   Drawing the people you care about fills art with purpose and love.

You don't have to make your coloring realistic.

Every style of art is special and valuable and can bring peace and
joy to the artist, as well as those who receive the art.

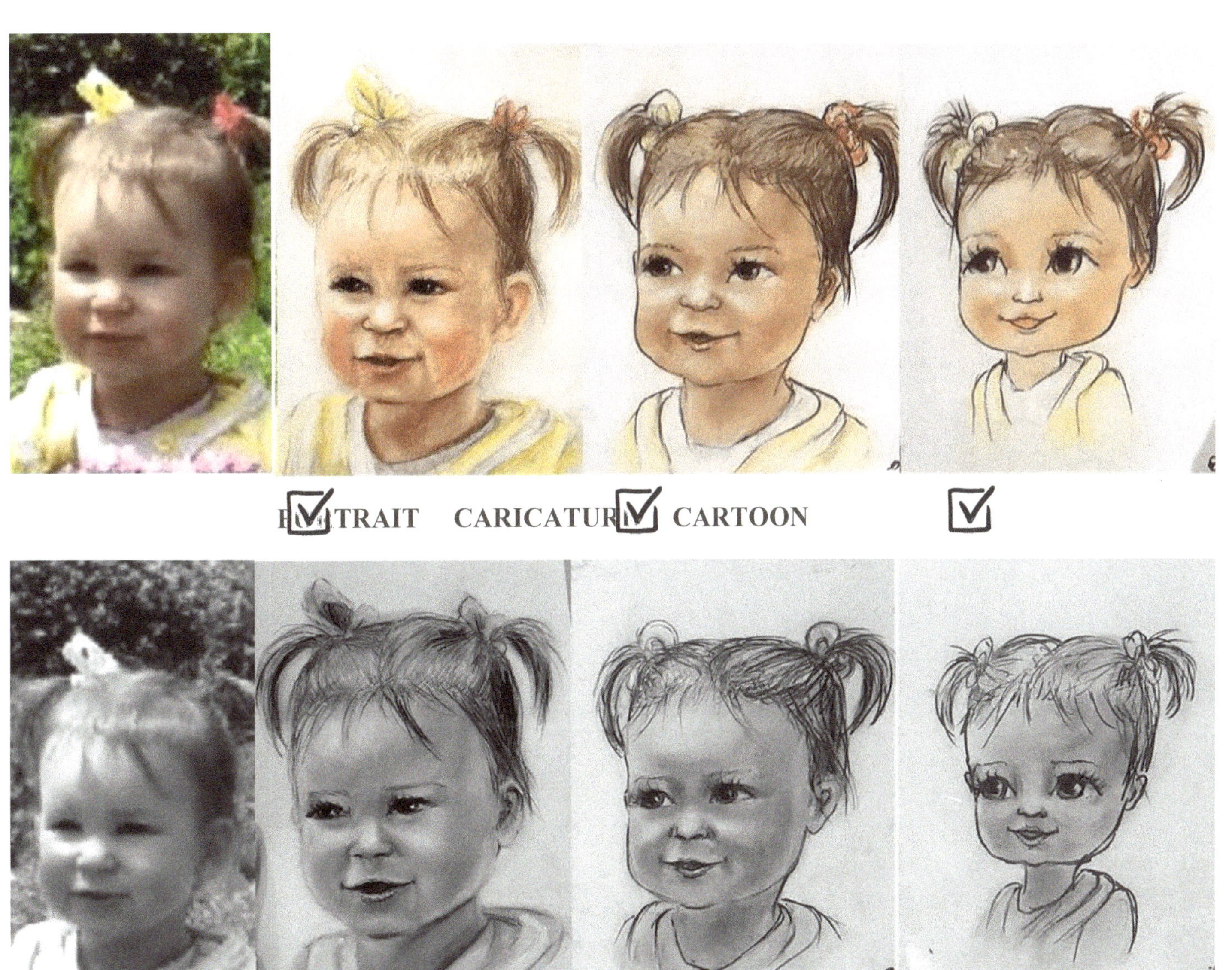

In coloring use hues that personally increase
your sense of joy.

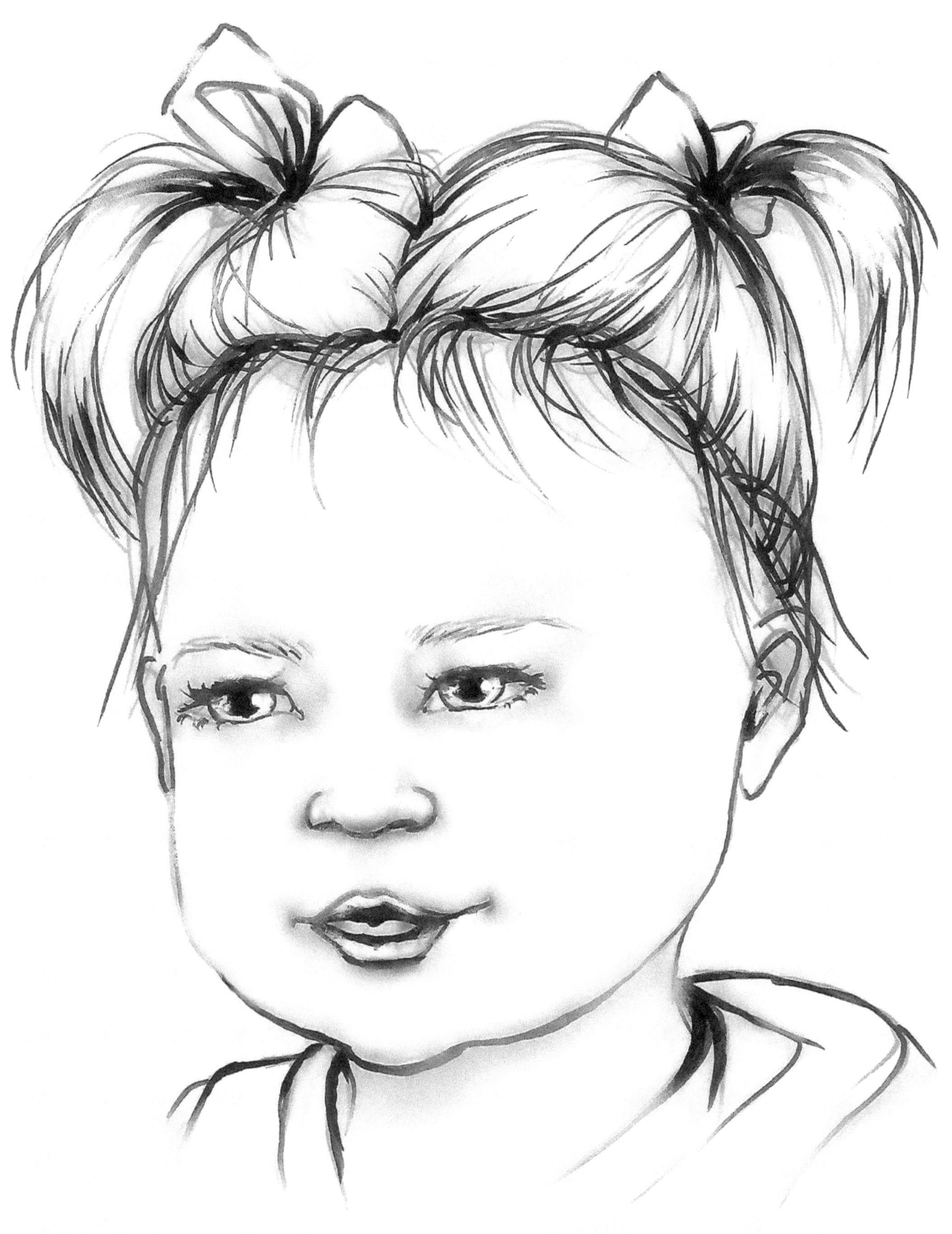

Trace

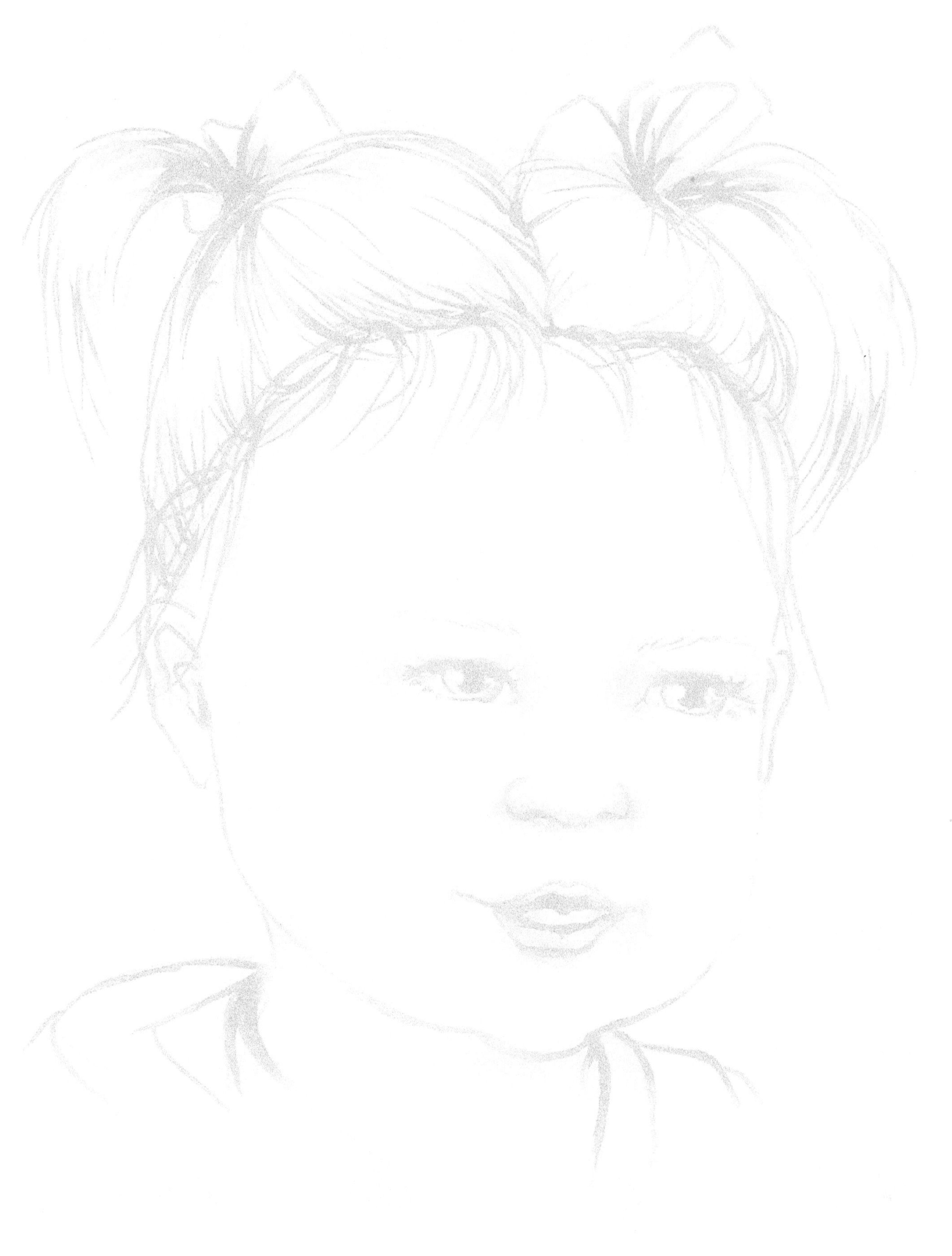

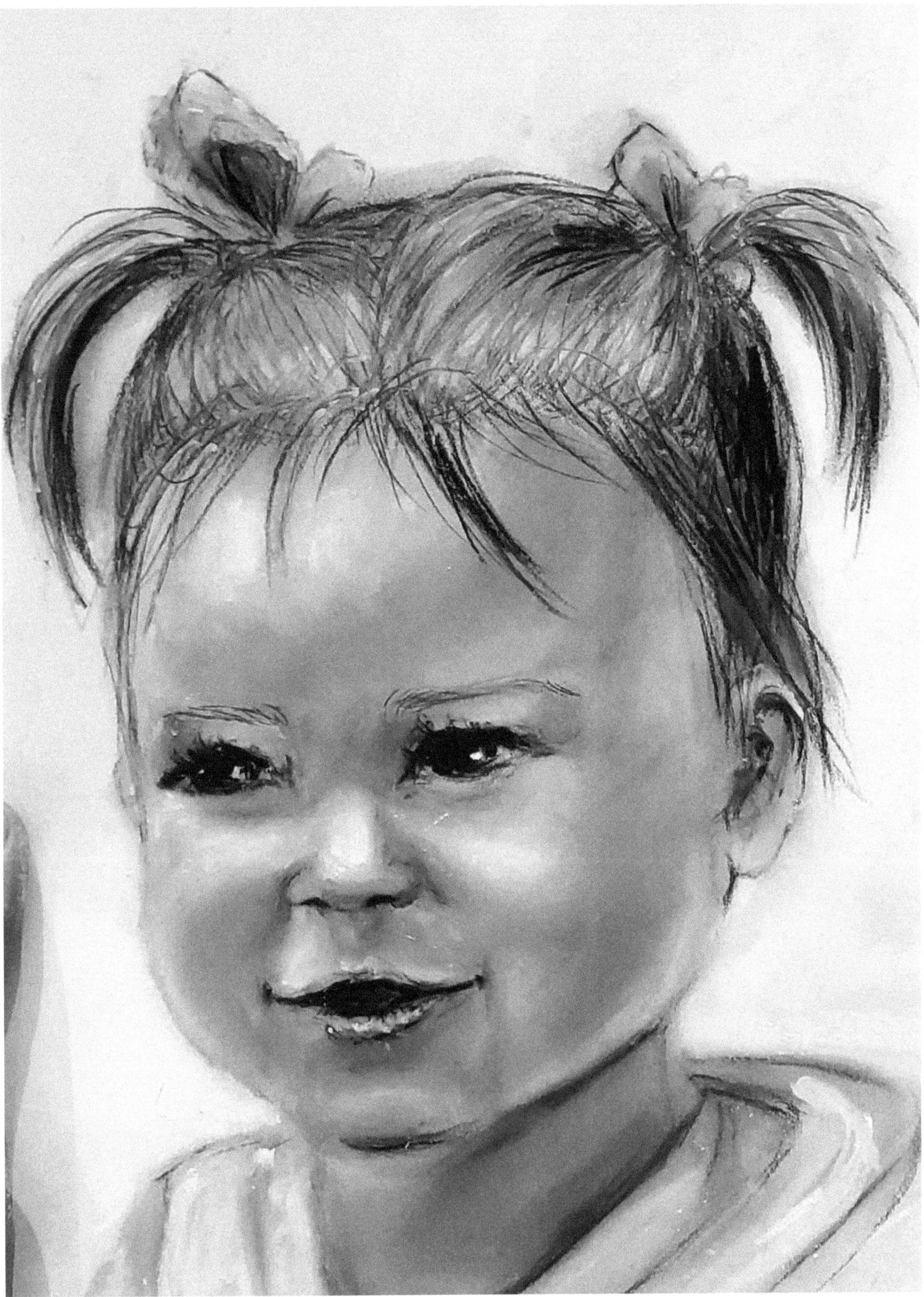

Art therapy occasionally utilized coloring pages. Imagine how beneficial it may be in art therapy to color images of happy babies.

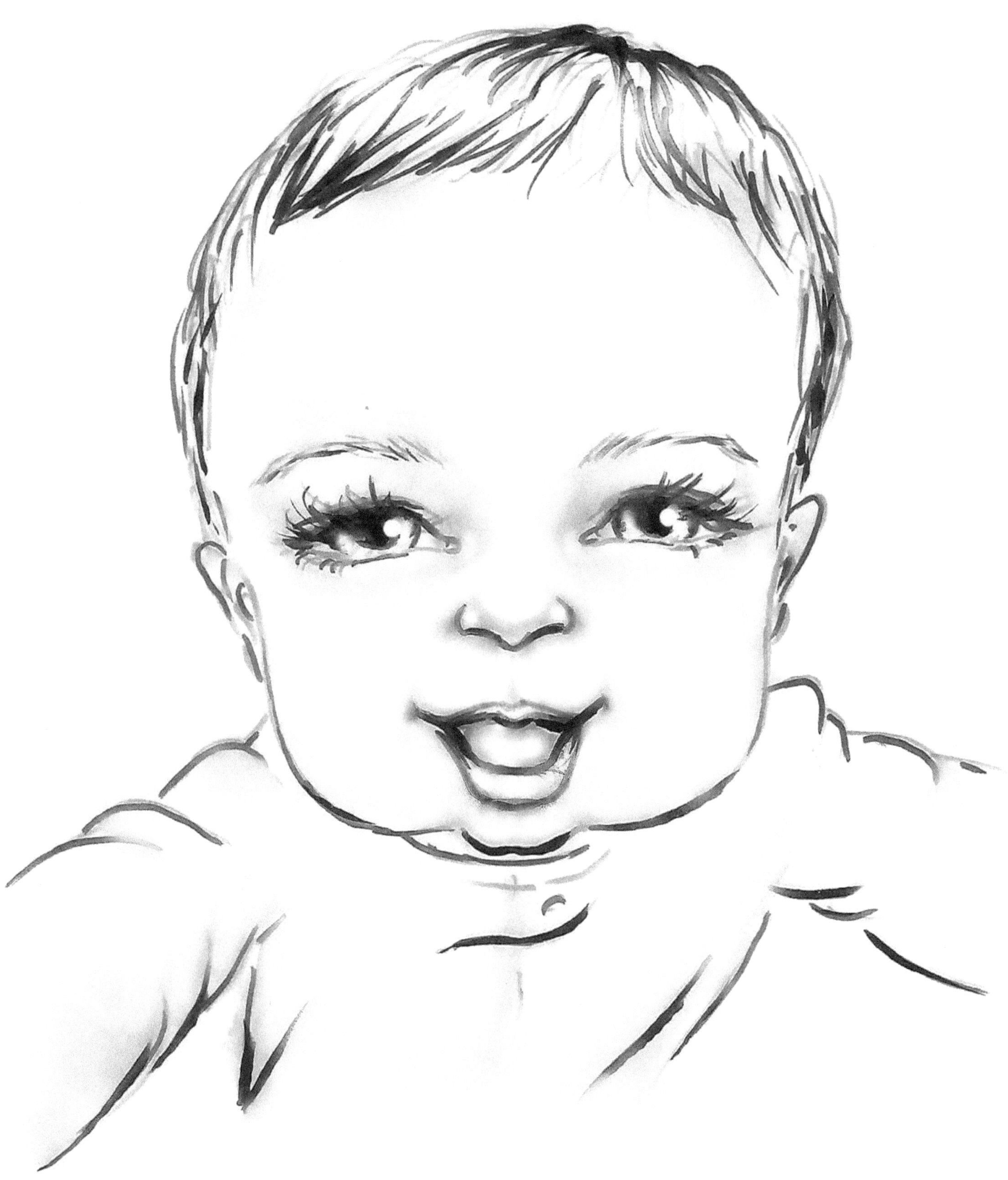
Color

Trace

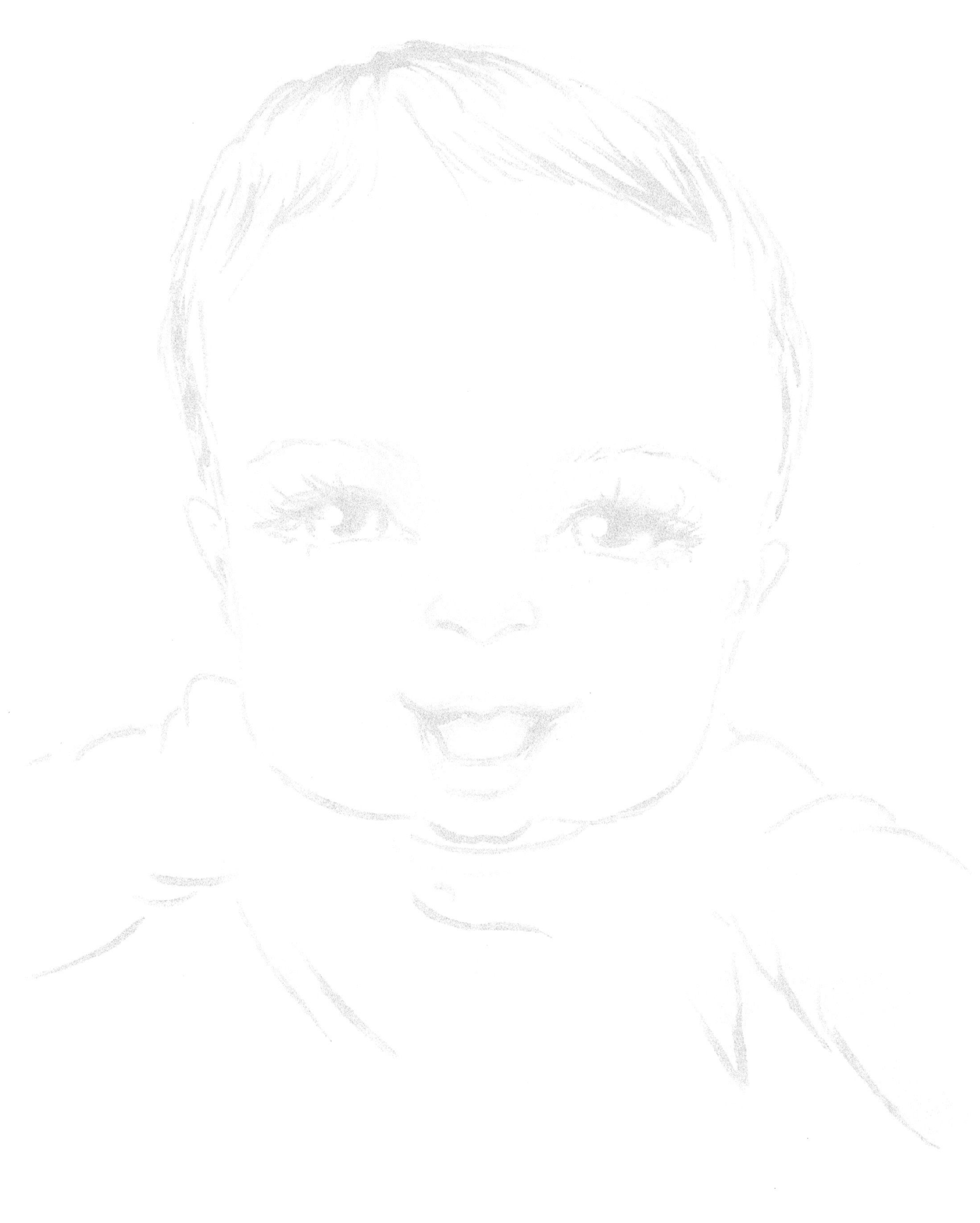

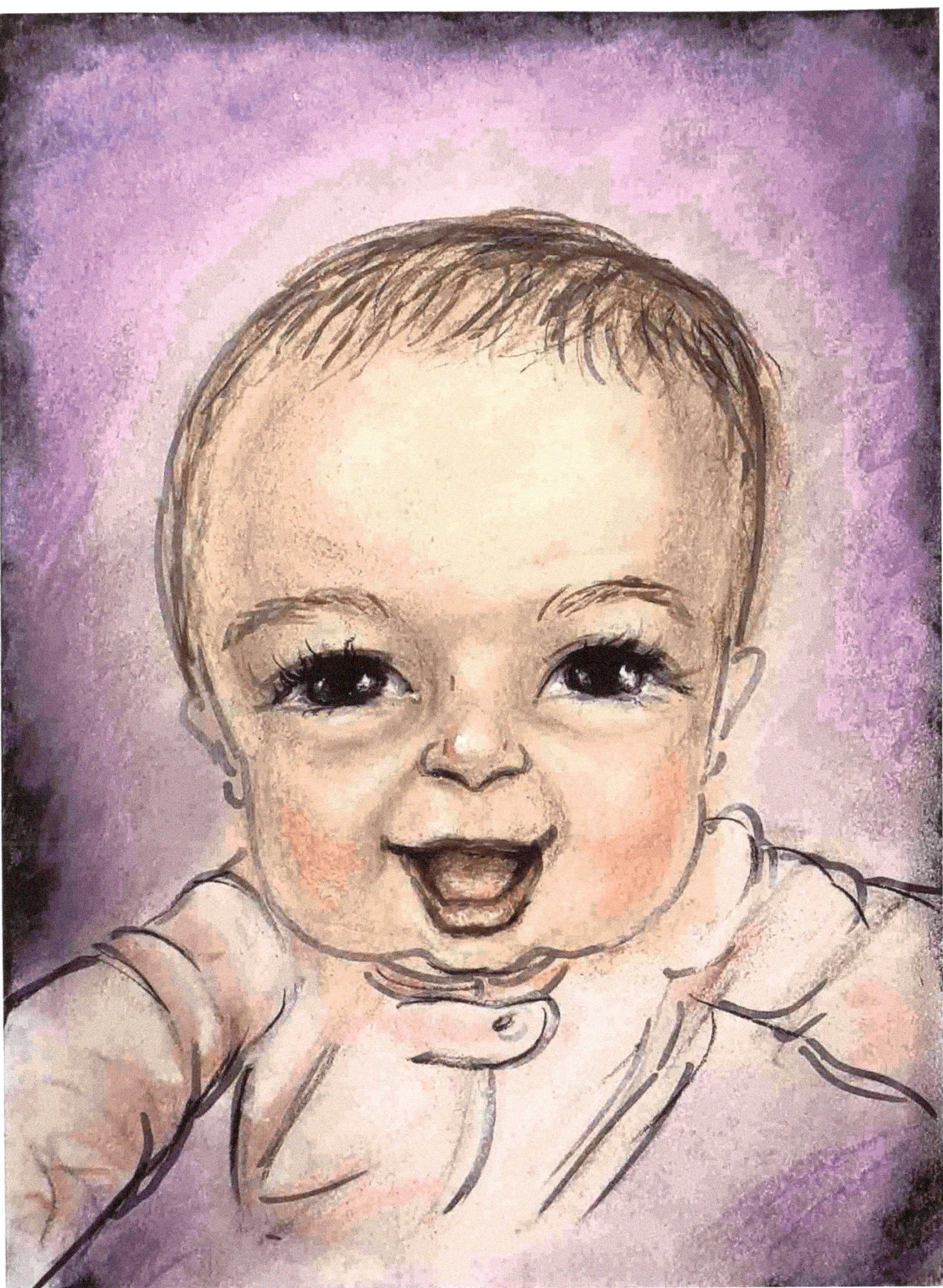

Enjoy your creative side, try coloring the eyes, hair, and
clothes a different color than in the original artwork.

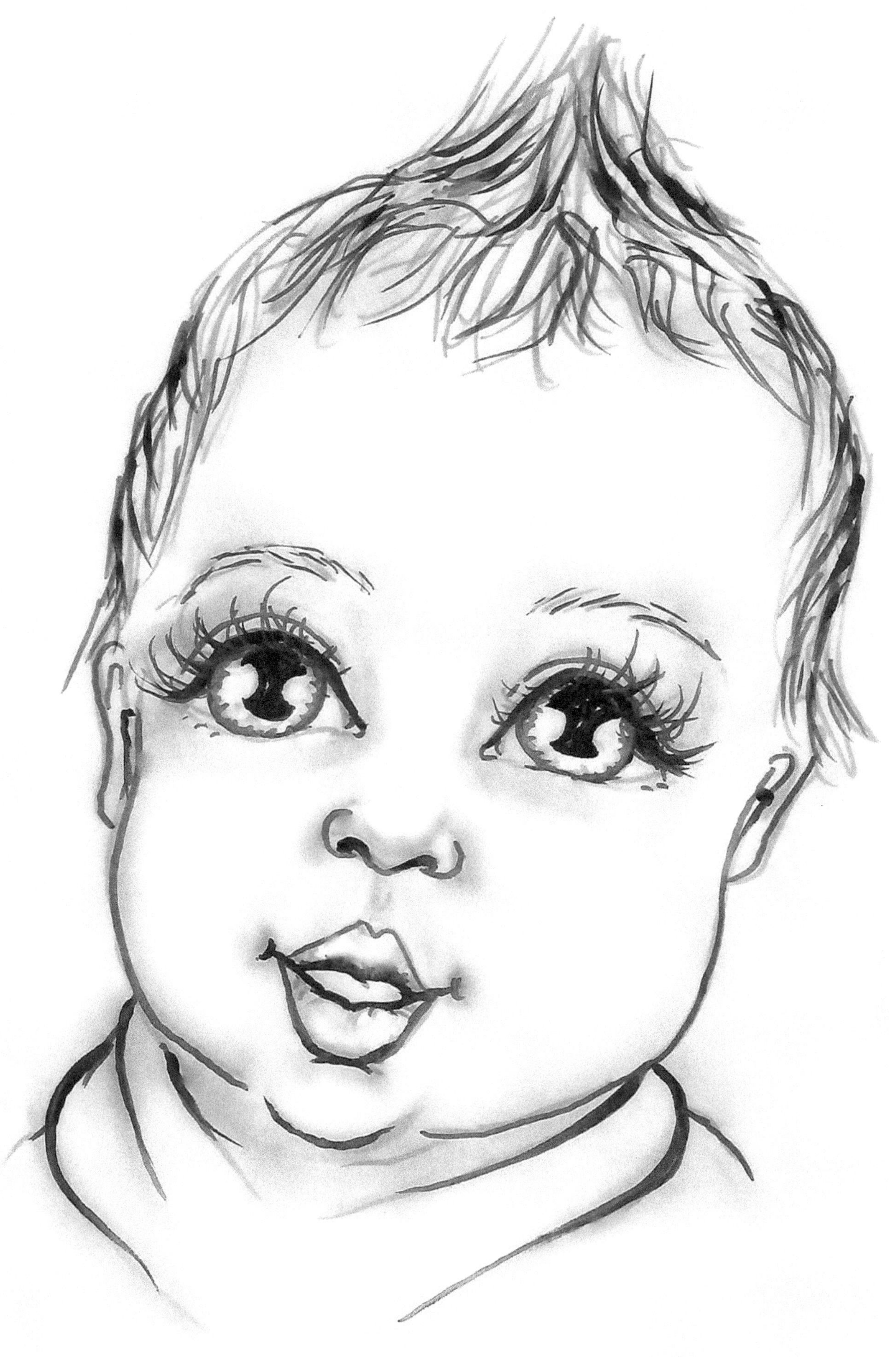
Color

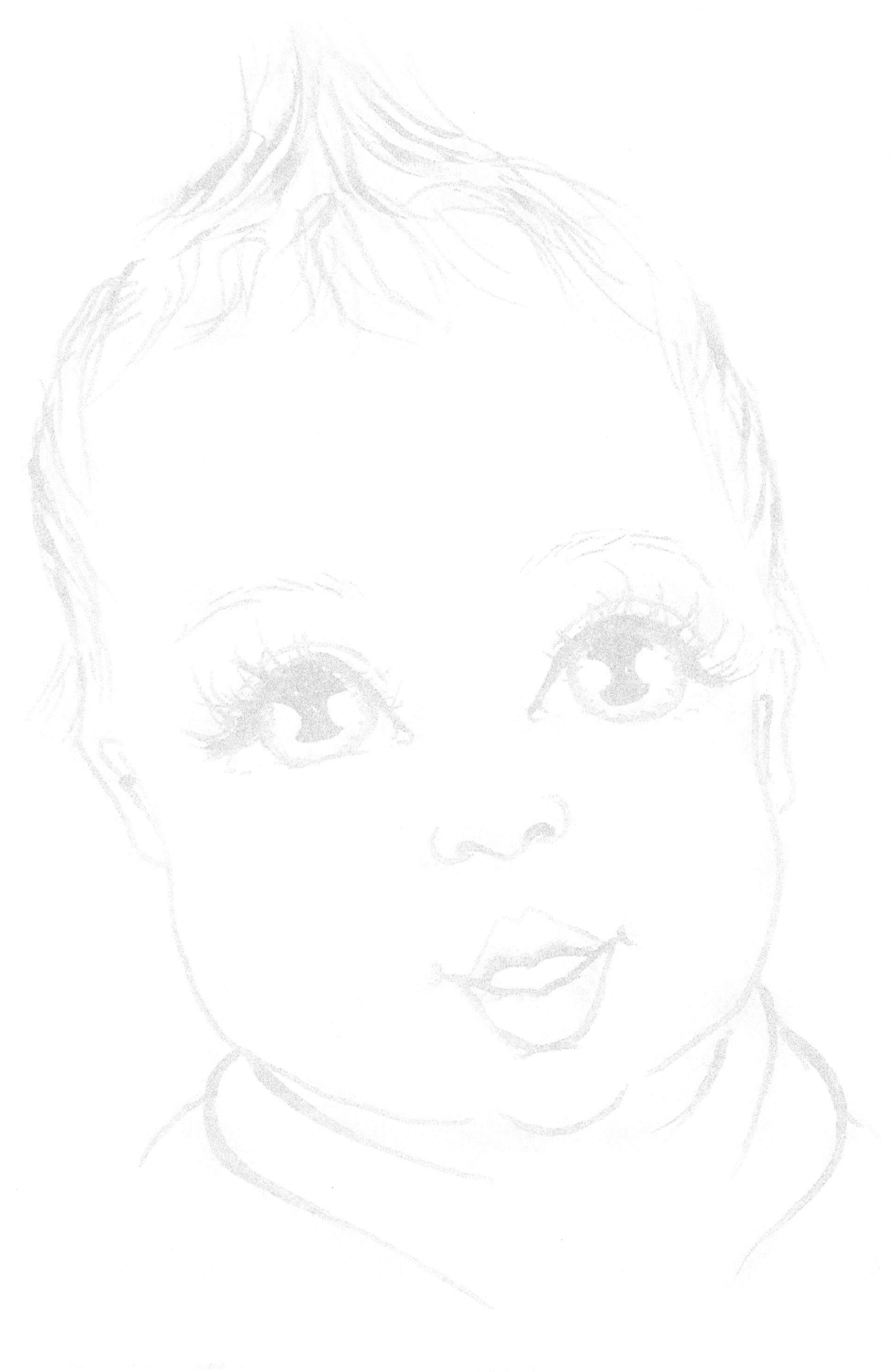

Trace

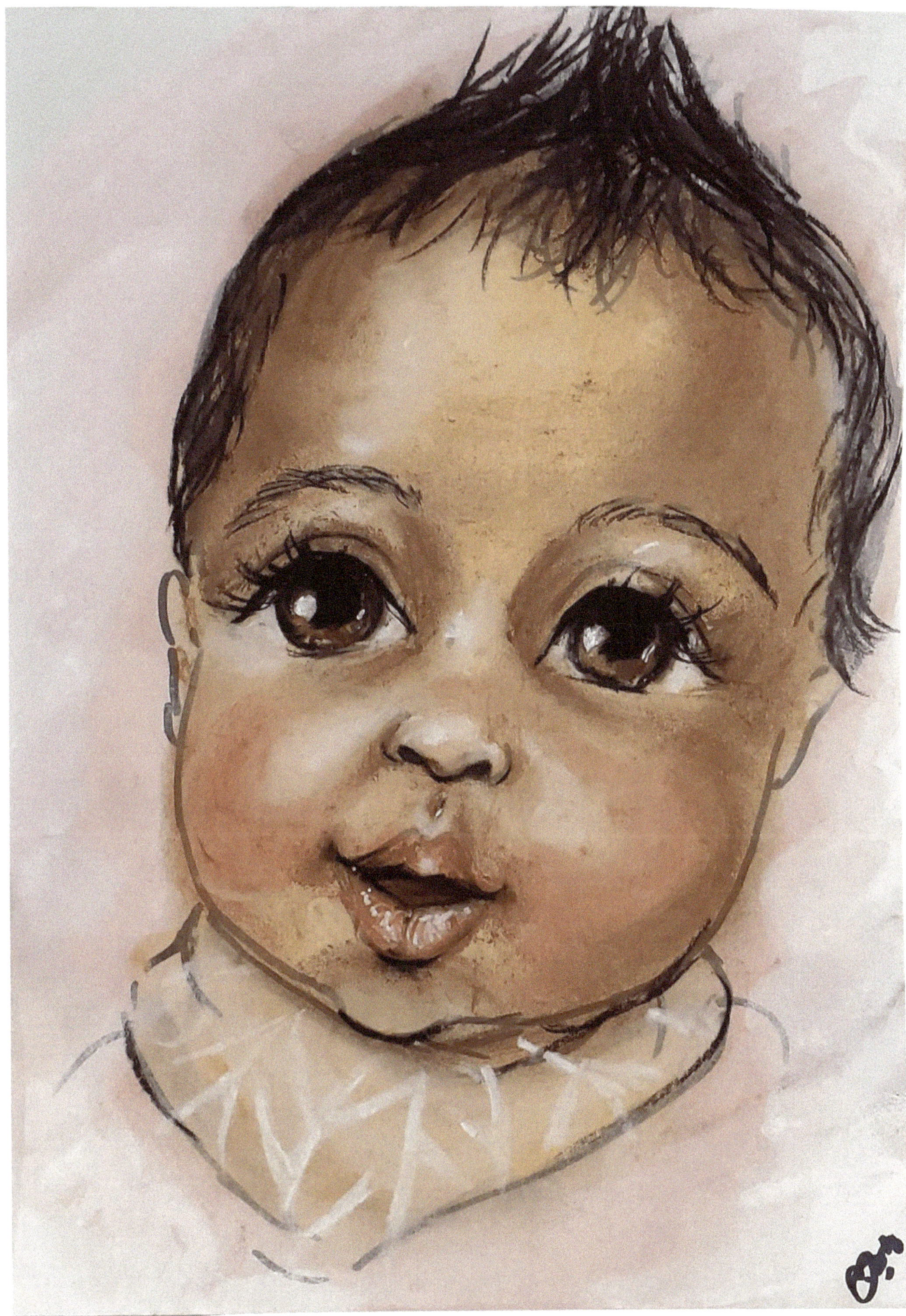

It is easier to identify light and shadow areas in monochromatic coloring. Grayscale portraits, caricatures, and cartoons have a unique, classical feel to them.

Color

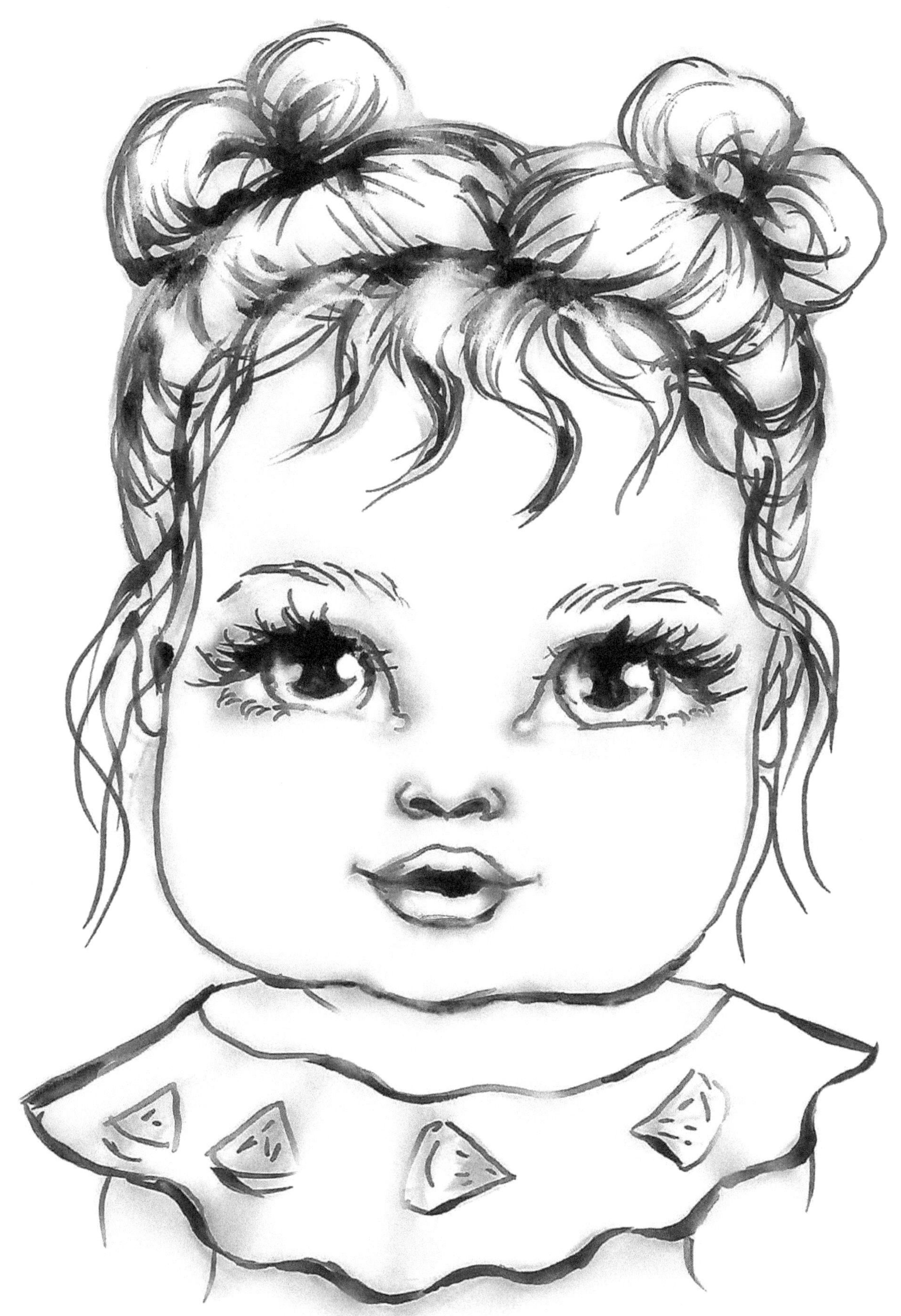

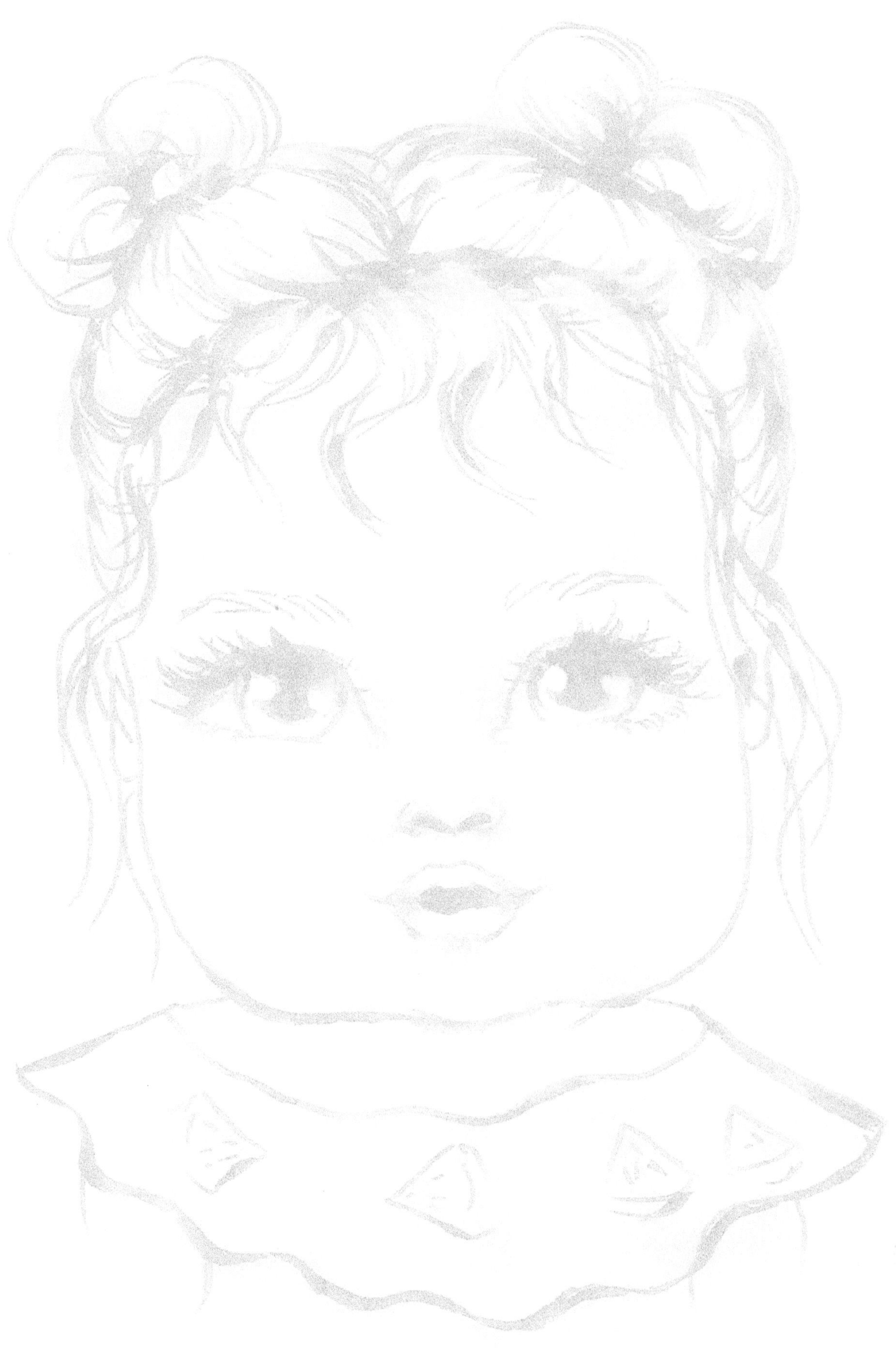

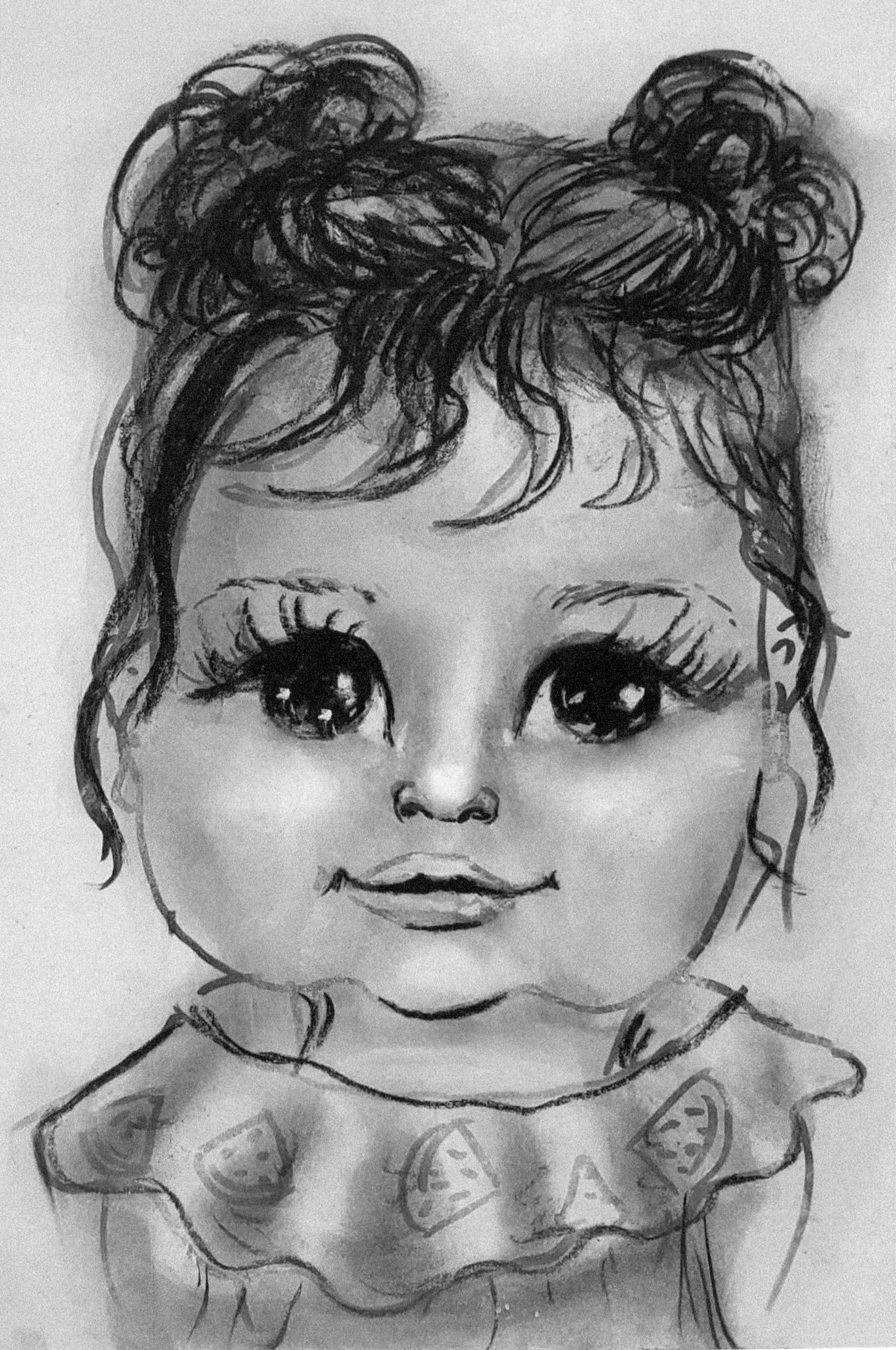

Try coloring using different dry media: colored pencils, charcoal, and soft pastels. Try mixing different drawing media. Feel free to experiment with different art materials.

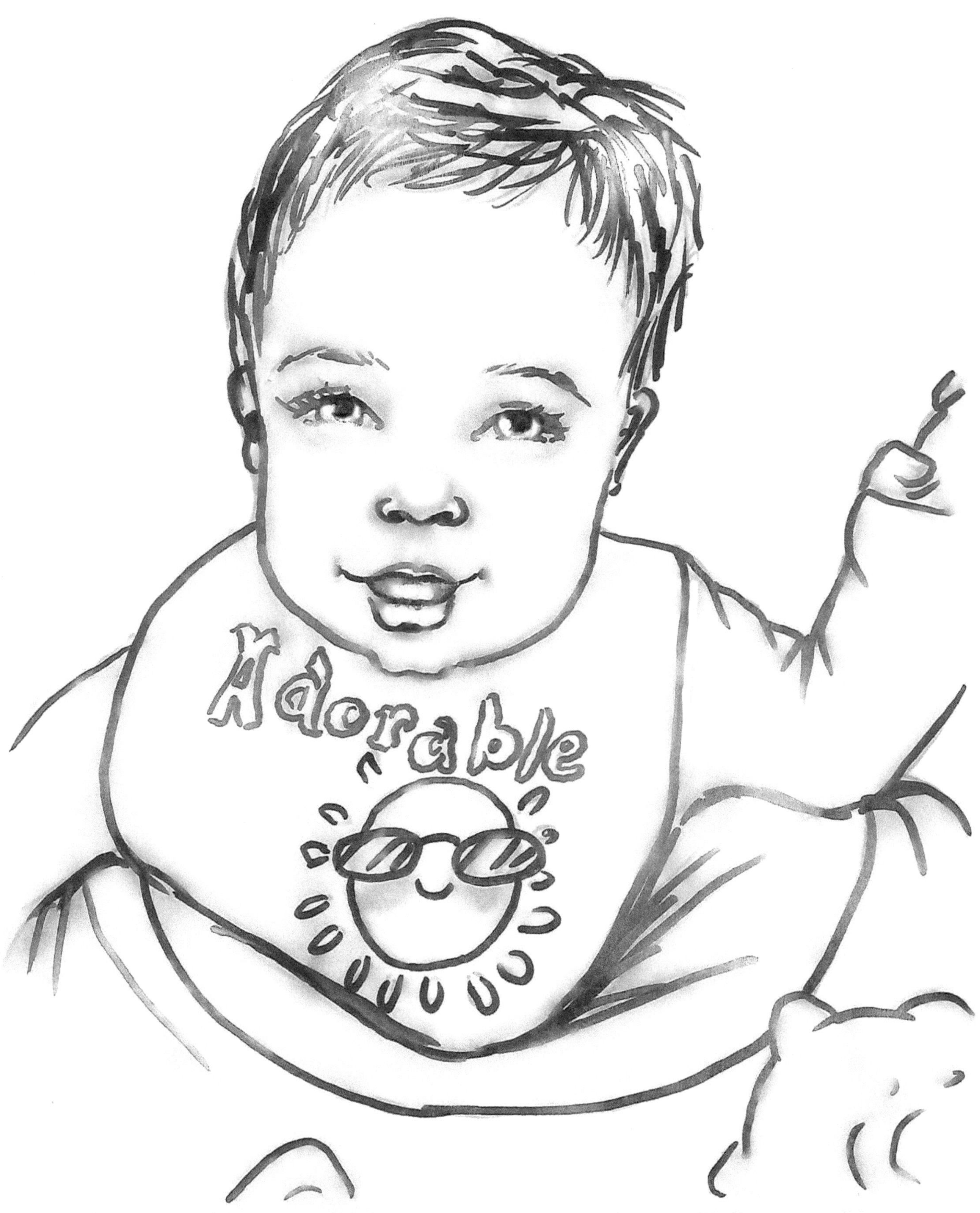
Adorable

Trace

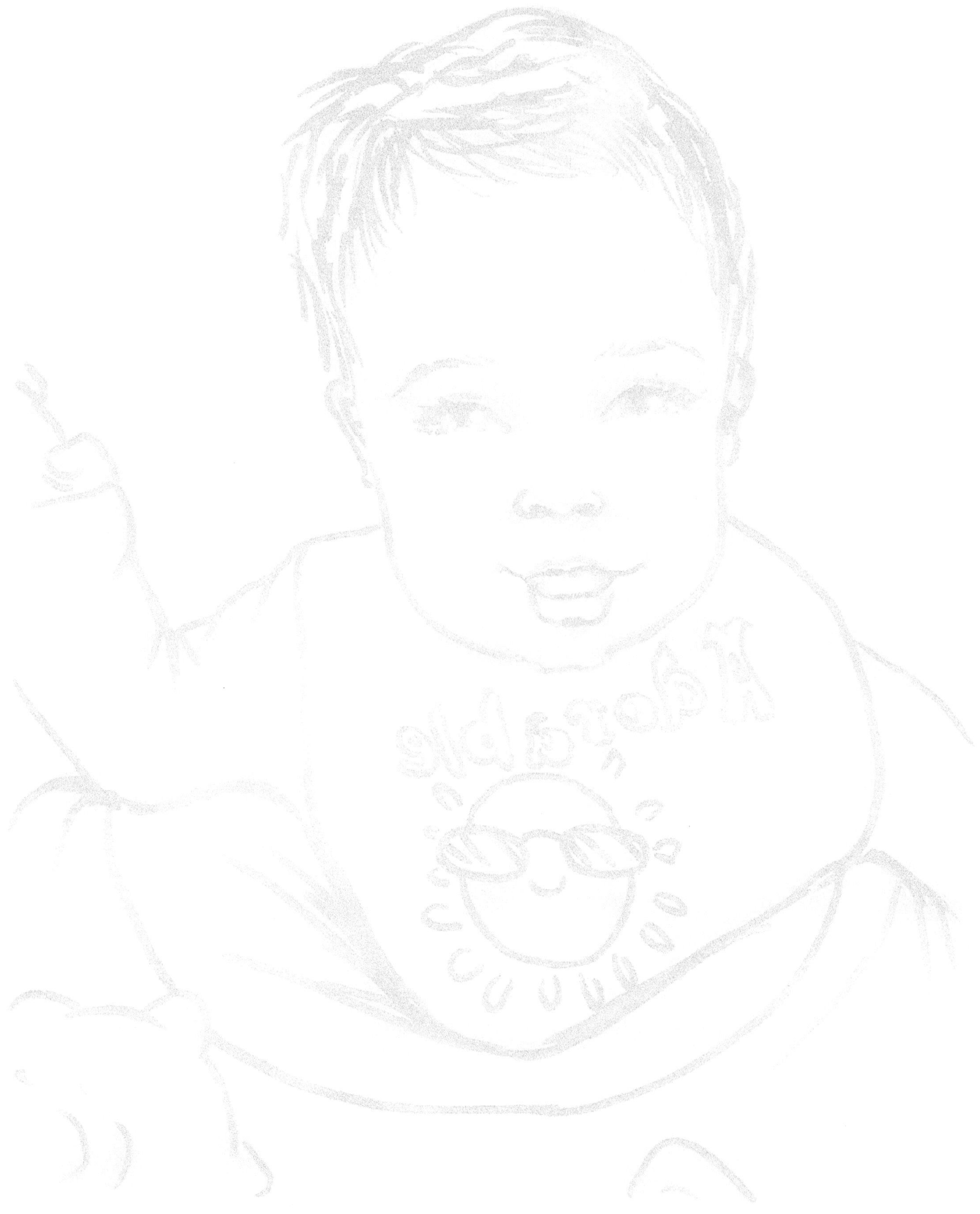

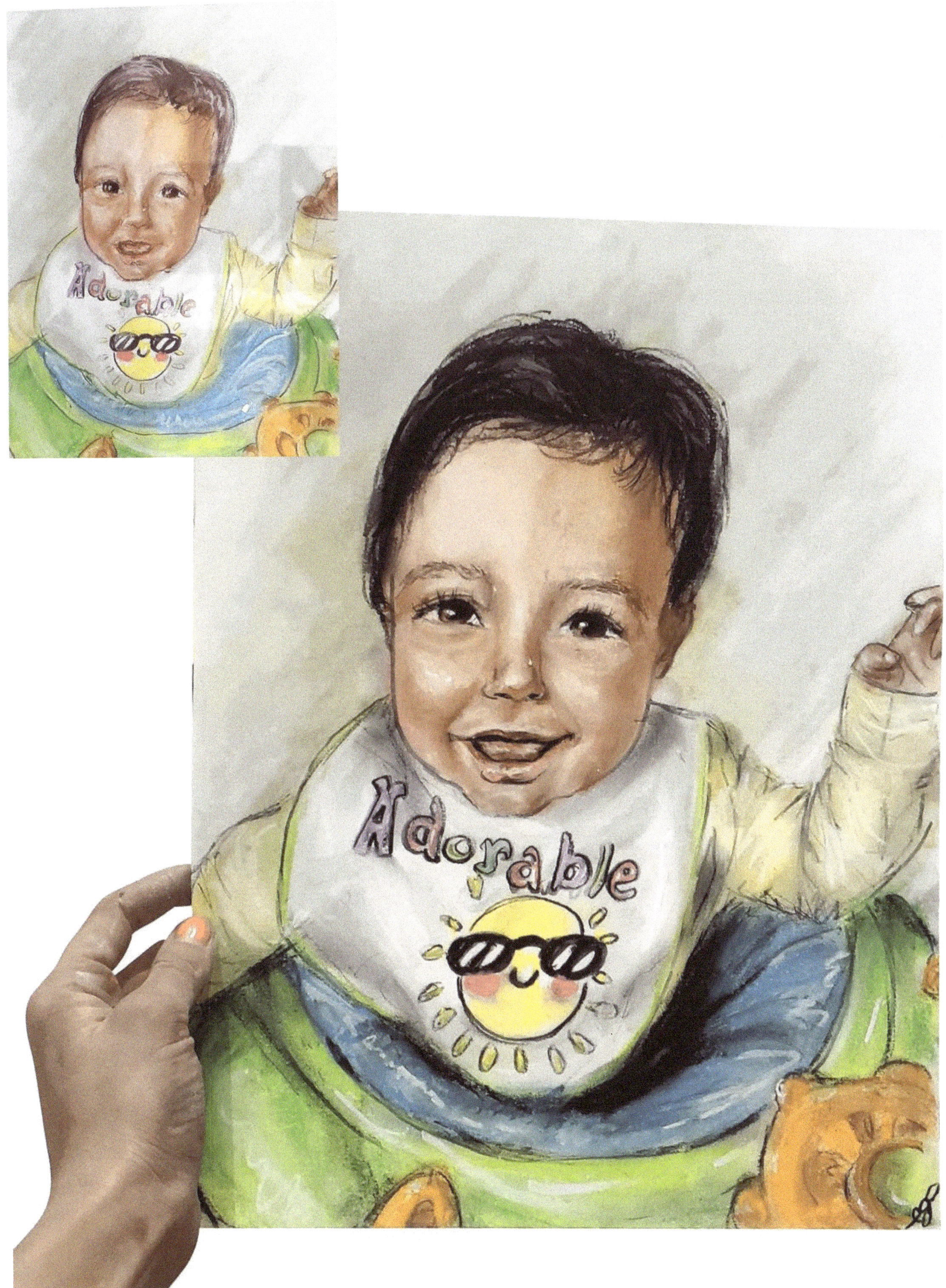

Adorable

Leave your cares behind and enjoy coloring
adorable happy babies.

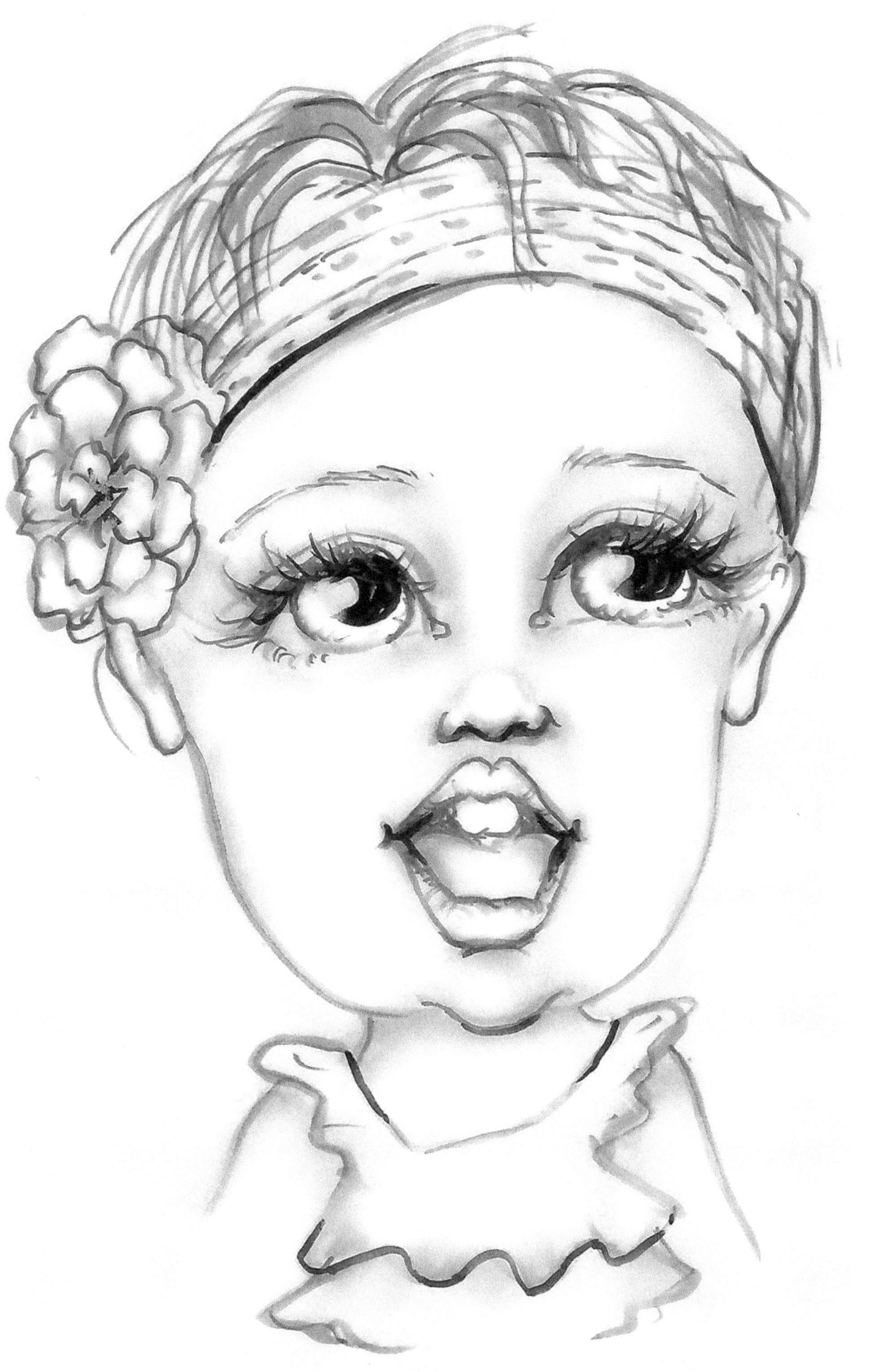
Color

Trace

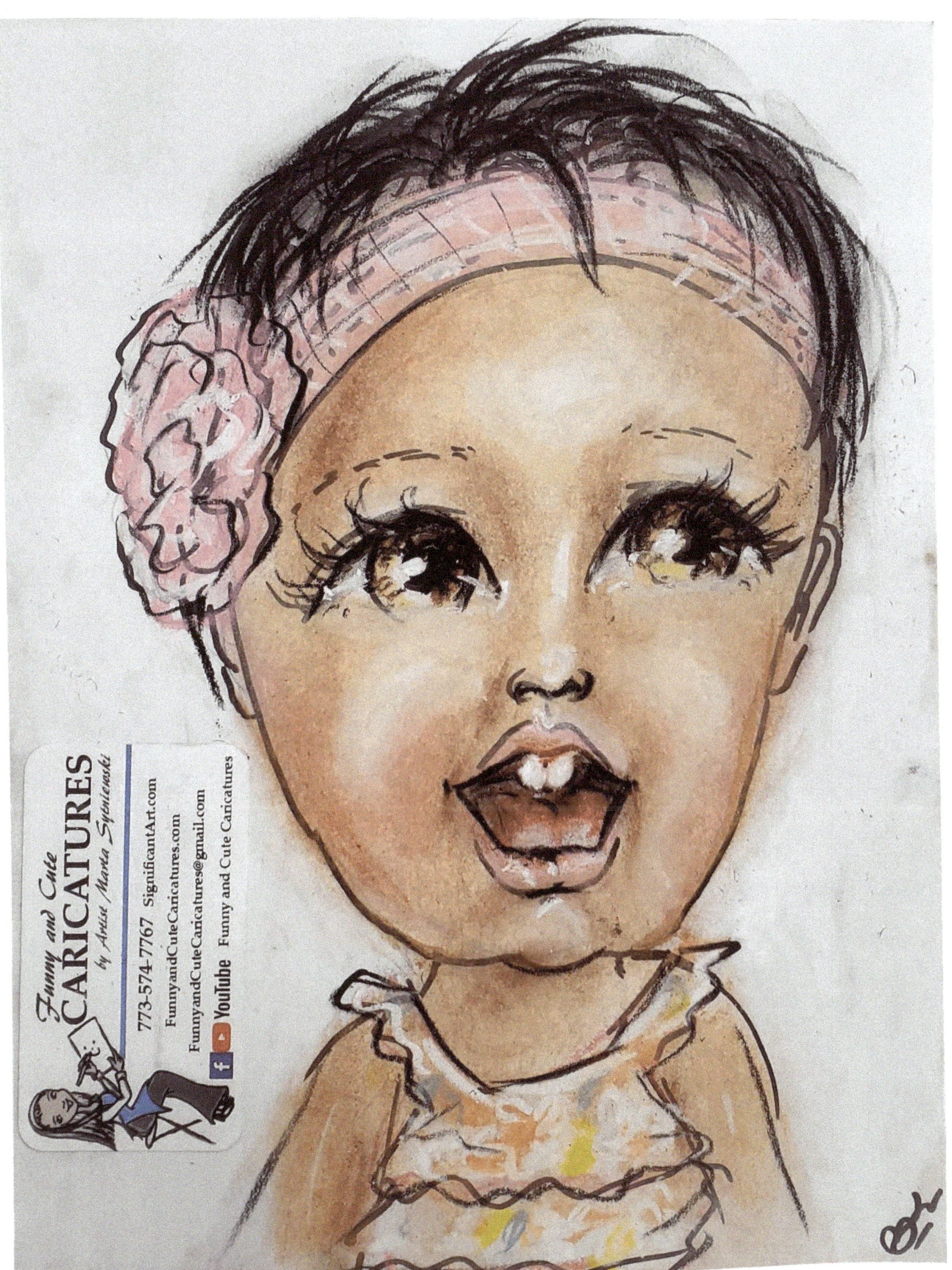
Funny and Cute
CARICATURES
by Artist Marta Sytniewski
773-574-7767 SignificantArt.com
FunnyandCuteCaricatures.com
FunnyandCuteCaricatures@gmail.com
f YouTube Funny and Cute Caricatures

Have fun coloring the background, try blending and
fading colors, creating different designs and patterns.

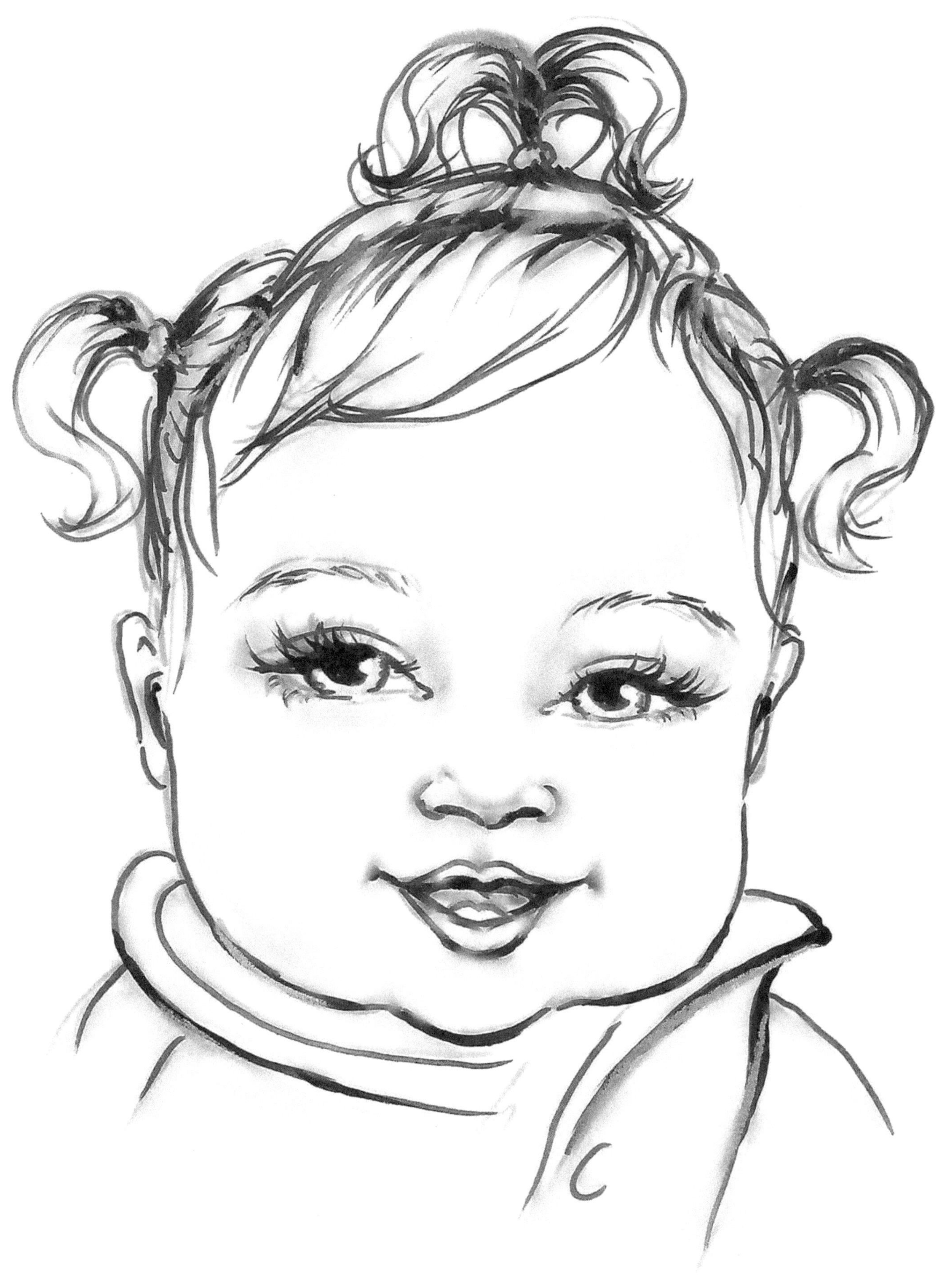

Color

Trace

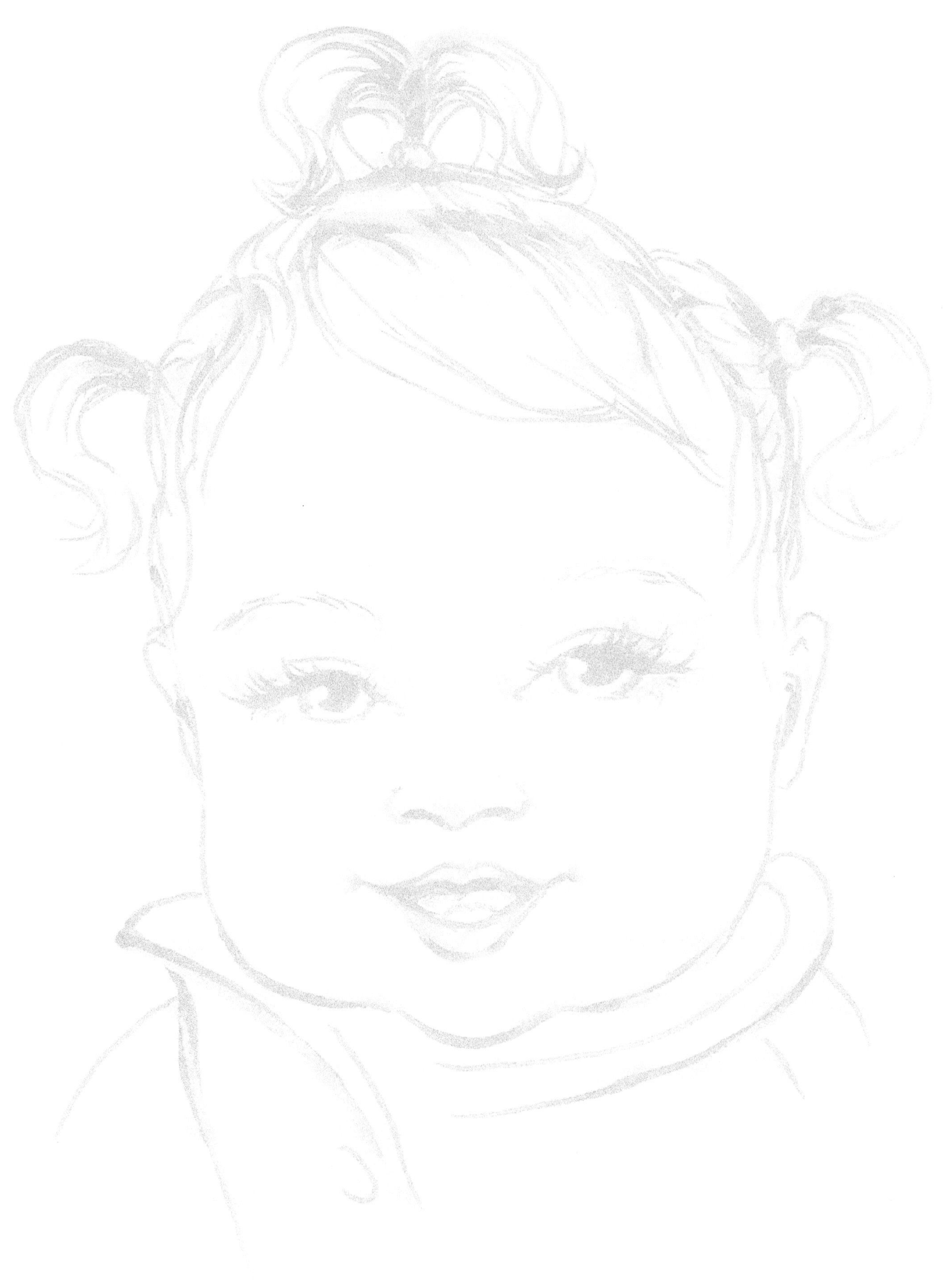

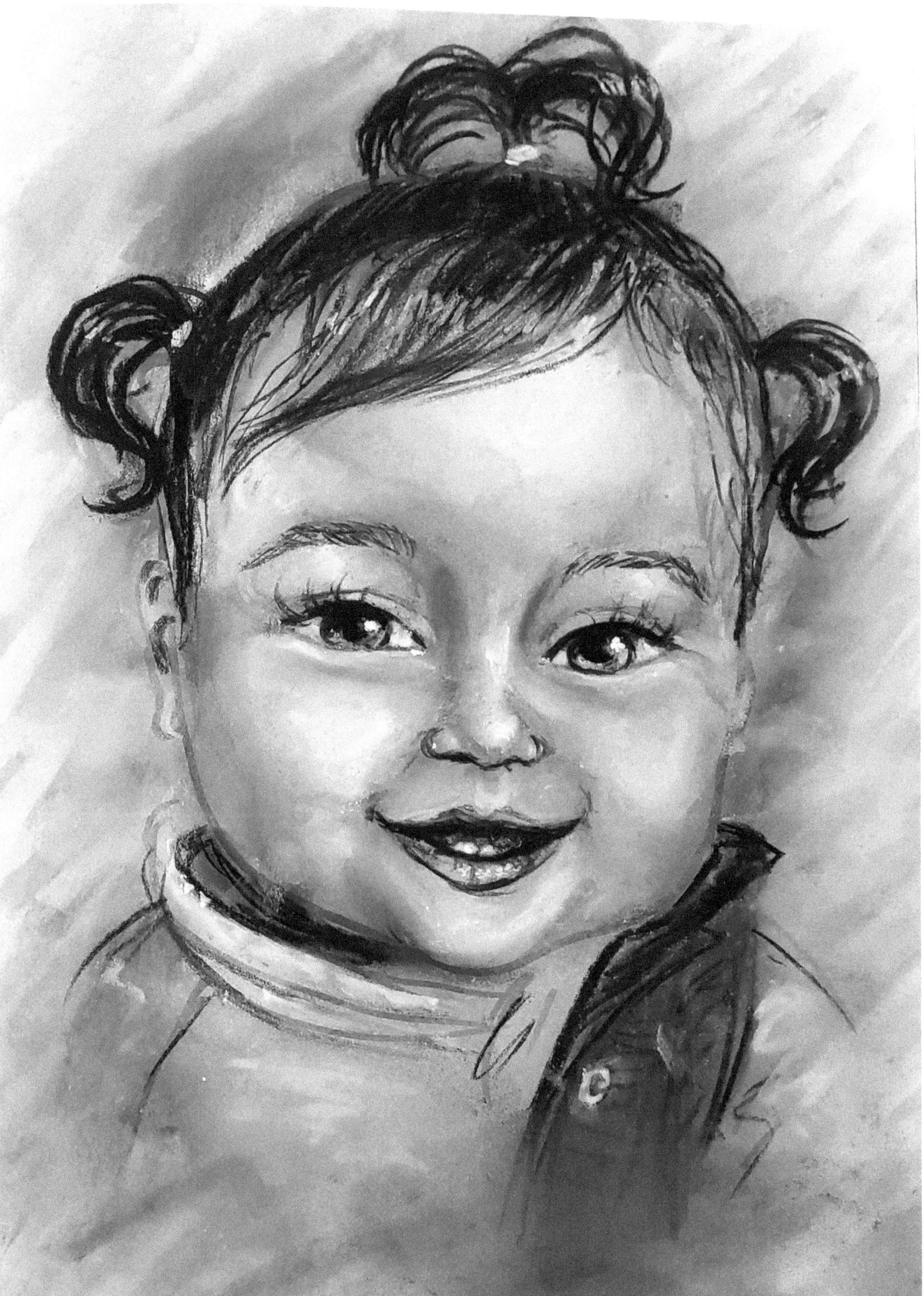

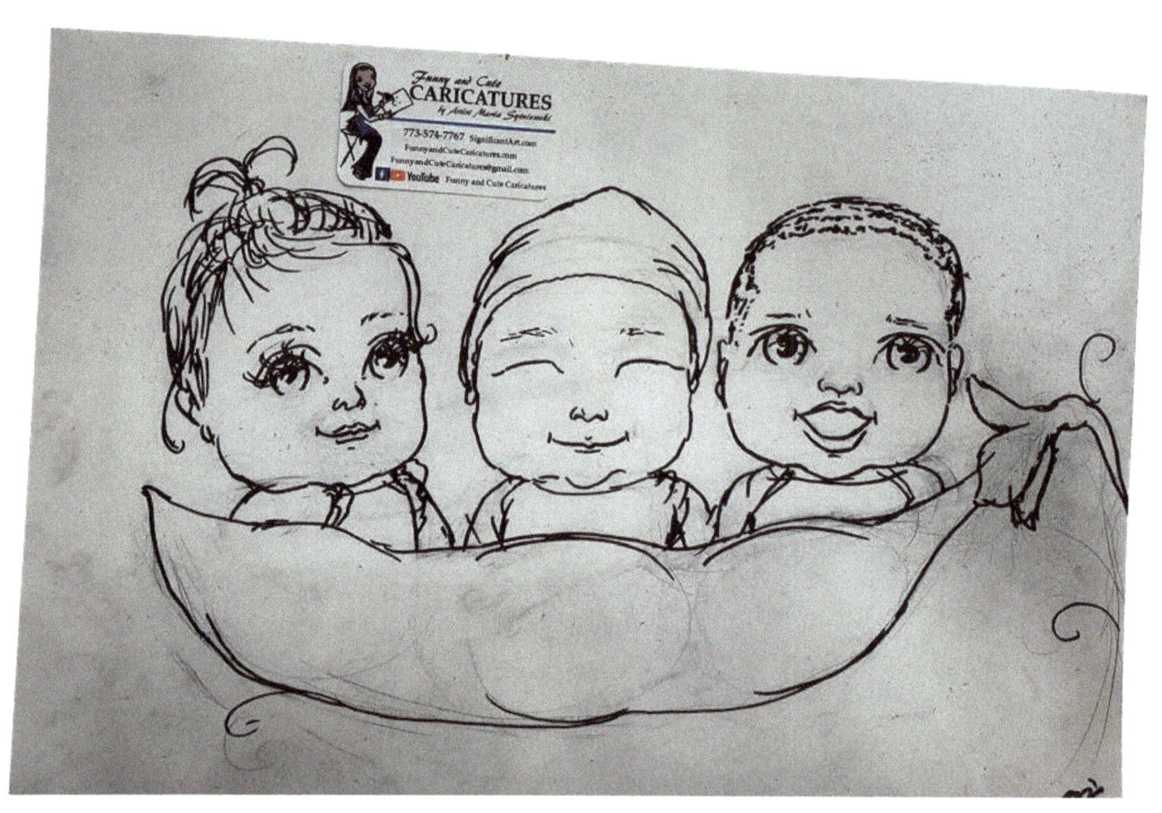

Funny and Cute
CARICATURES
by Anita Maria Szymianski
773-574-7767 SignificantArt.com
FunnyandCuteCaricatures.com
FunnyandCuteCaricatures@gmail.com
YouTube Funny and Cute Caricatures

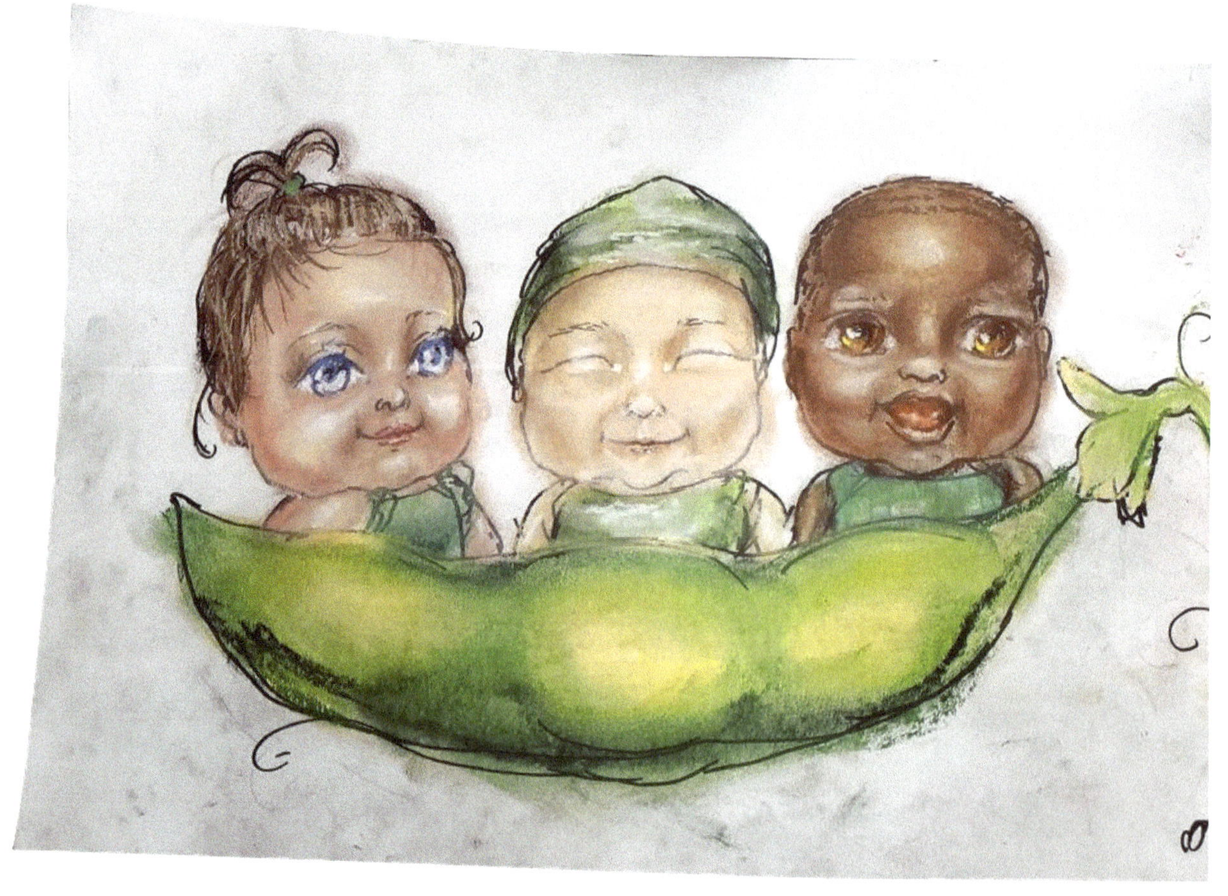

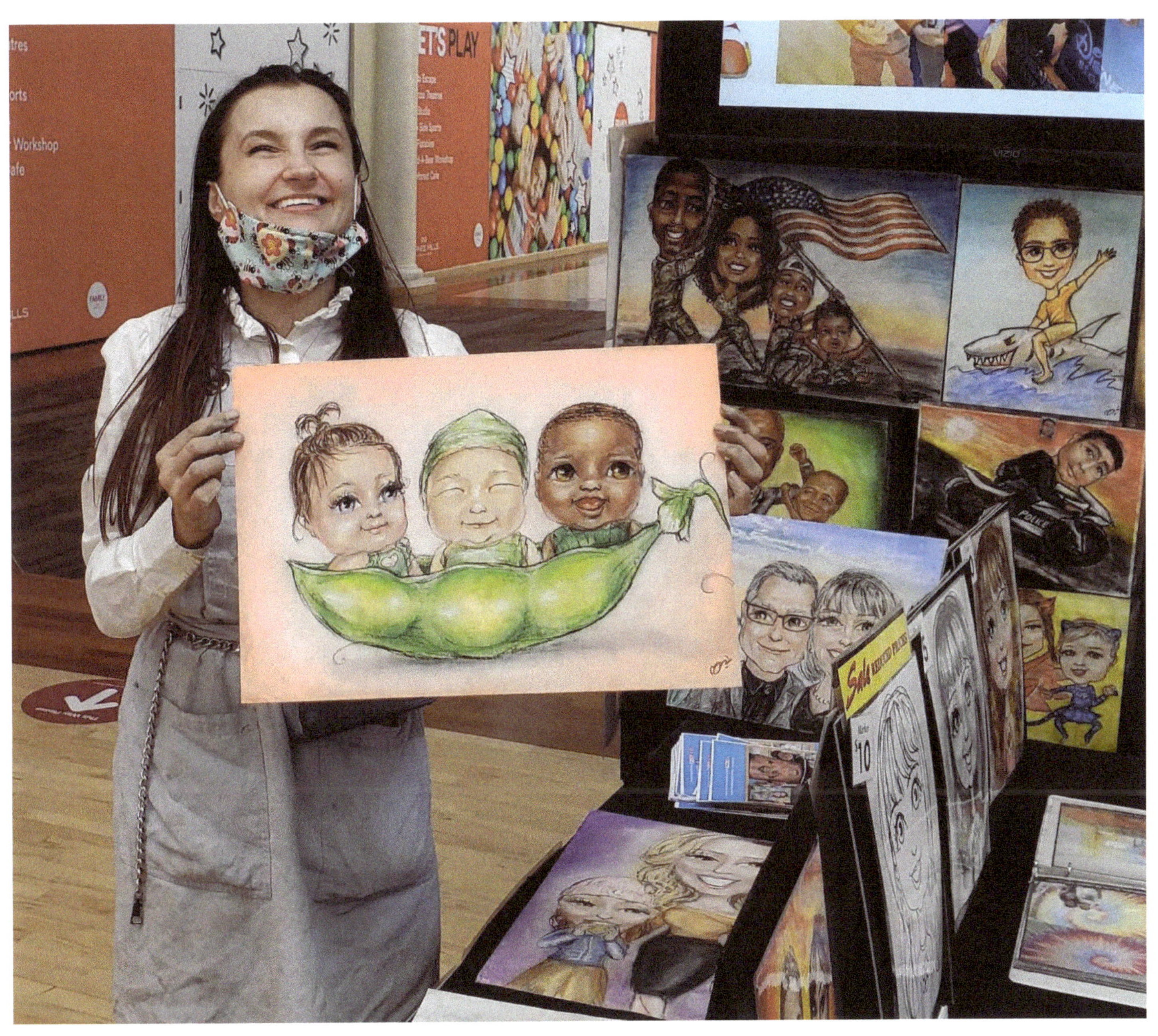

Try combining faces from different pictures into one unified drawing. In this example I drew multiracial babies, from different references, in one peapod together.

Drawing siblings is especially valuable because it illustrates their relationship. It is wonderful to see children happy together in works of art.

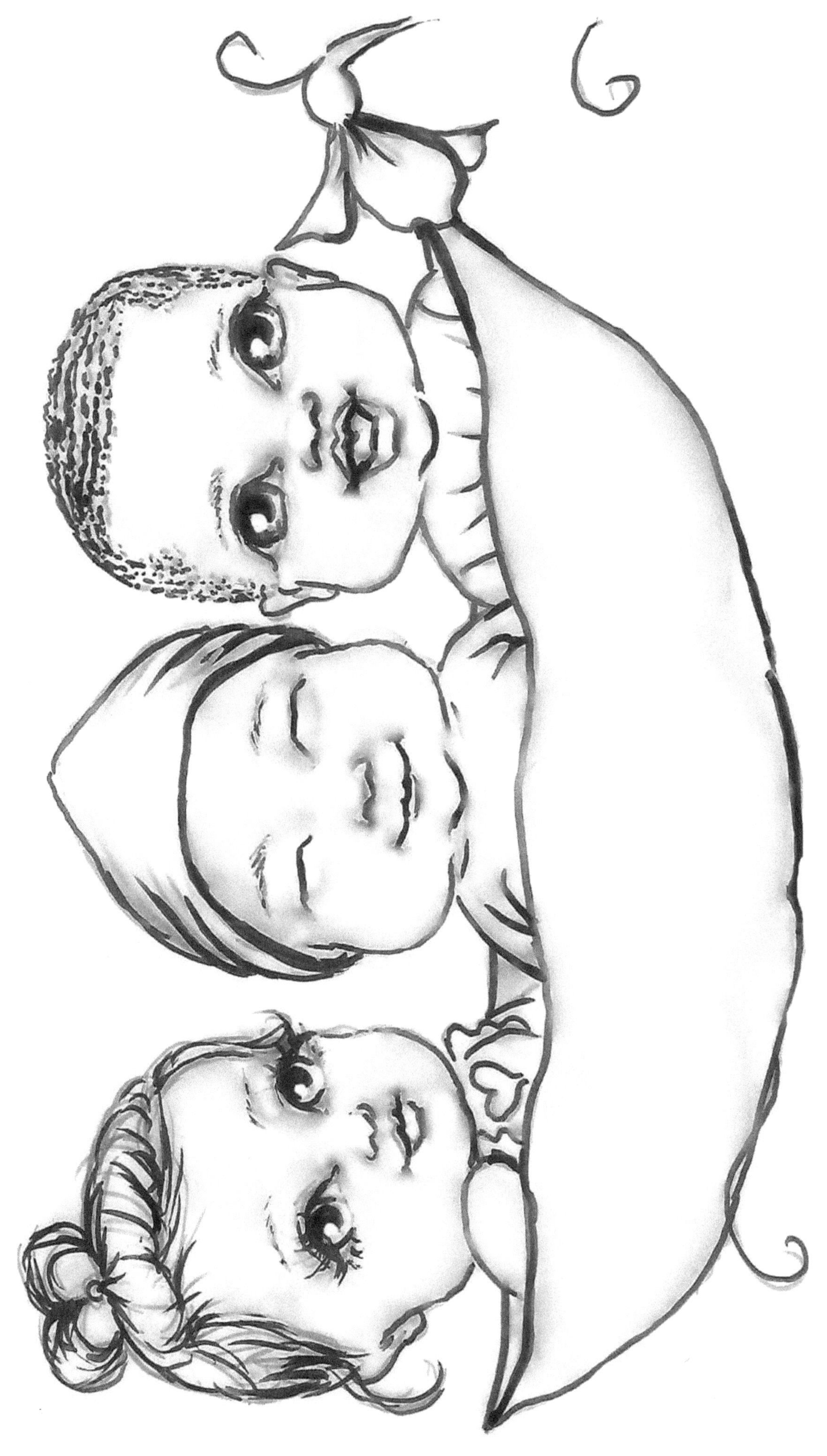

Trace

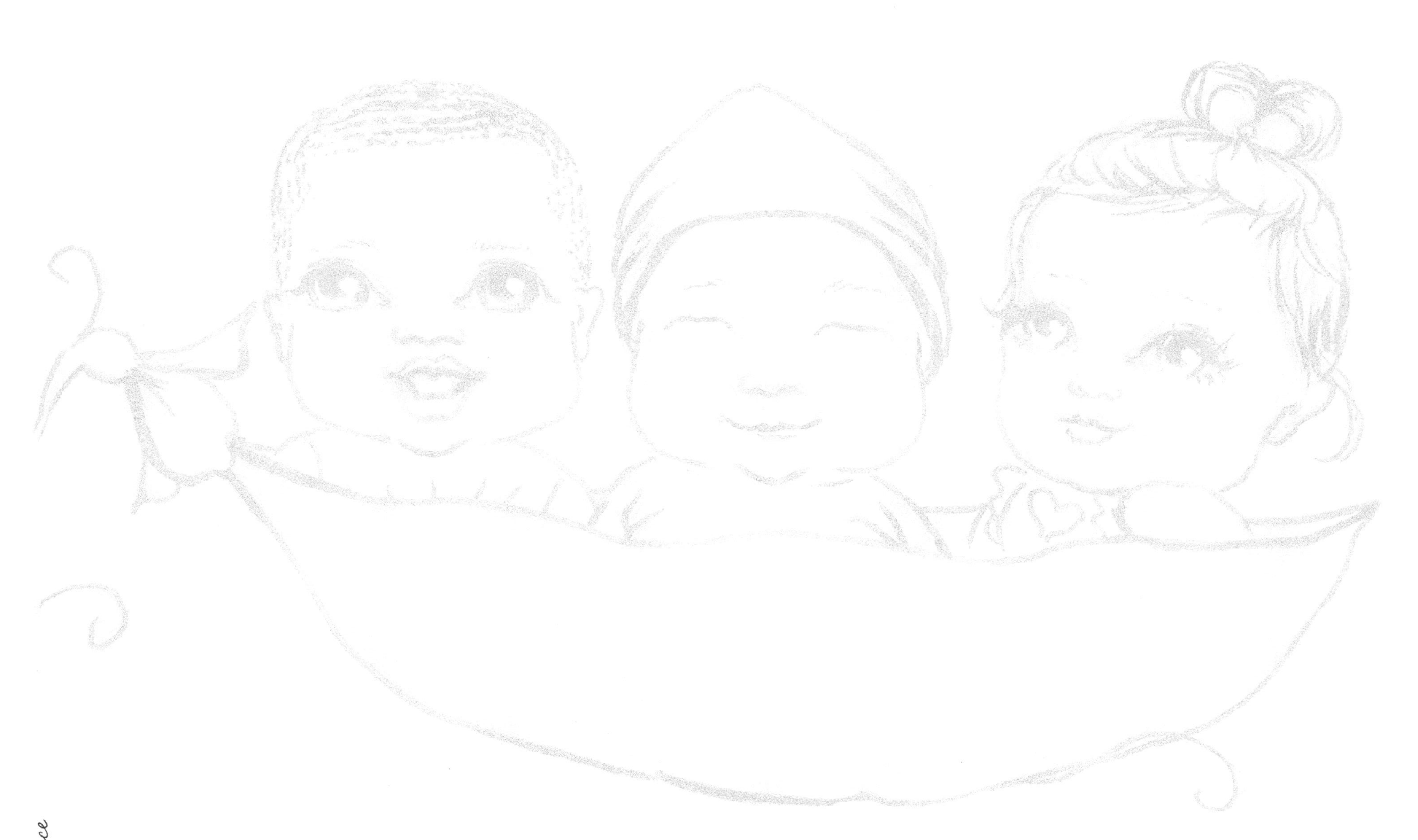

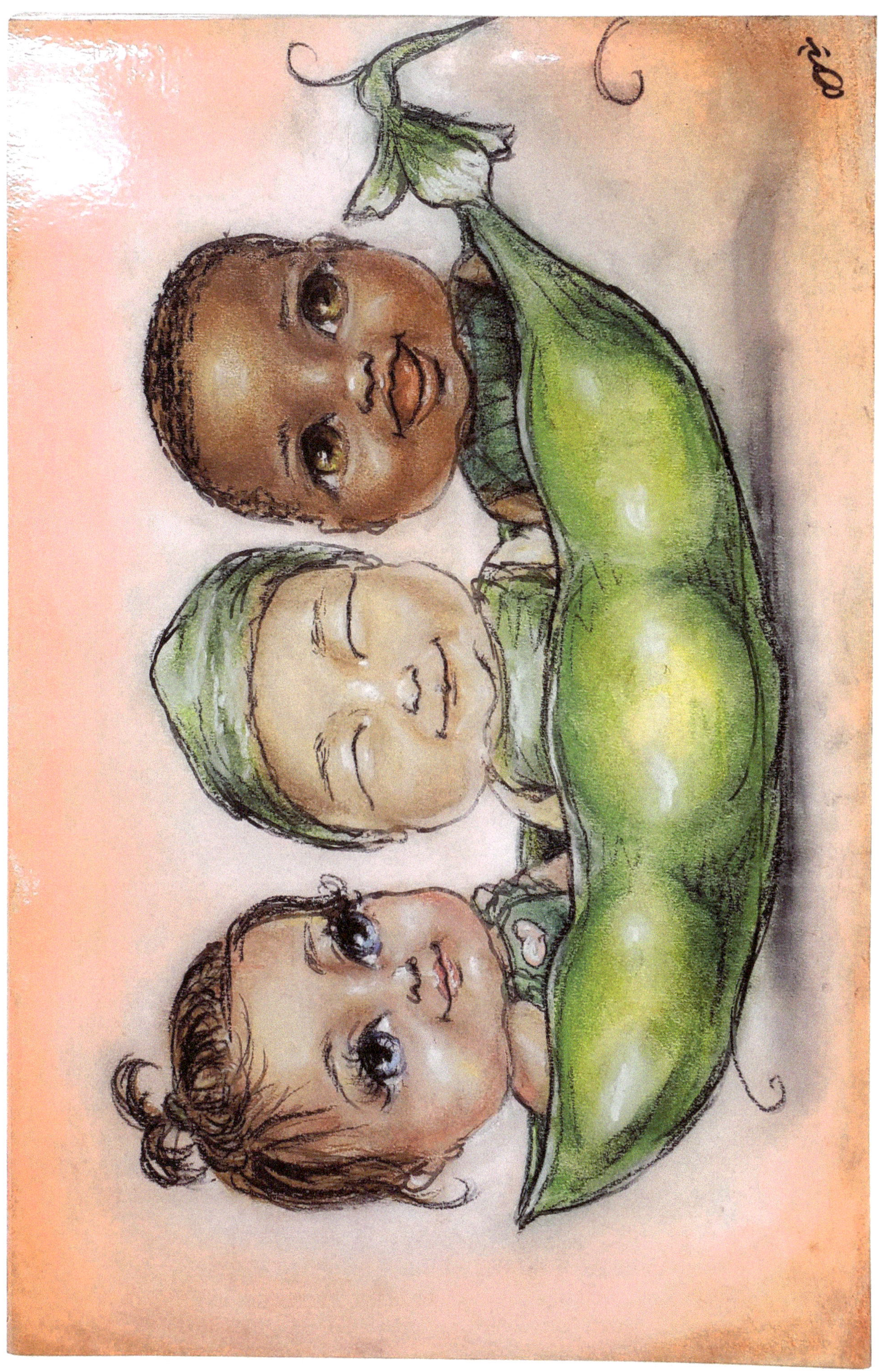

Learning how to draw can be accomplished
through practice, imitation, and observation. Practice
drawing on this page in addition to the coloring, tracing,
and observation pages already provided.

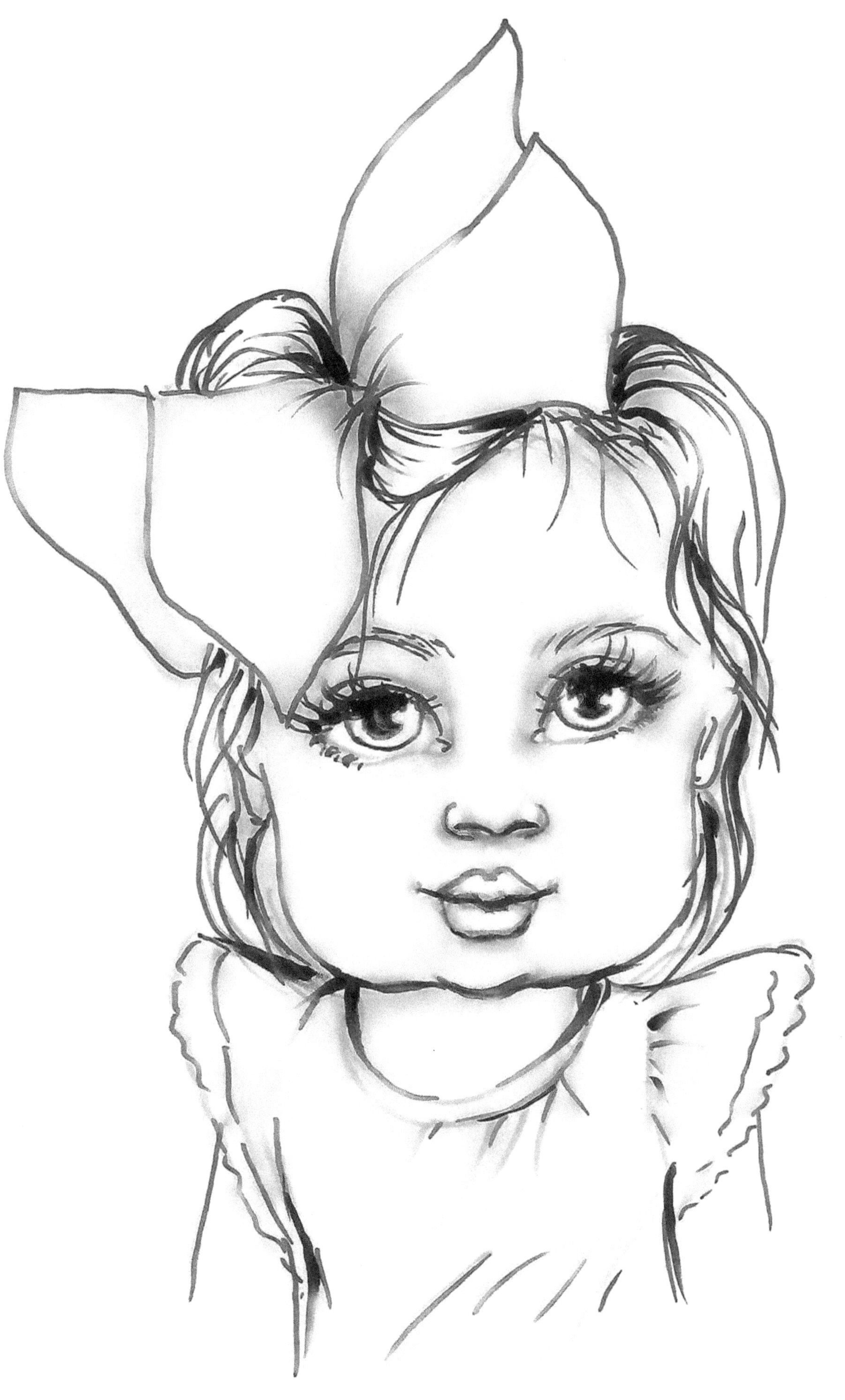
Color

Trace

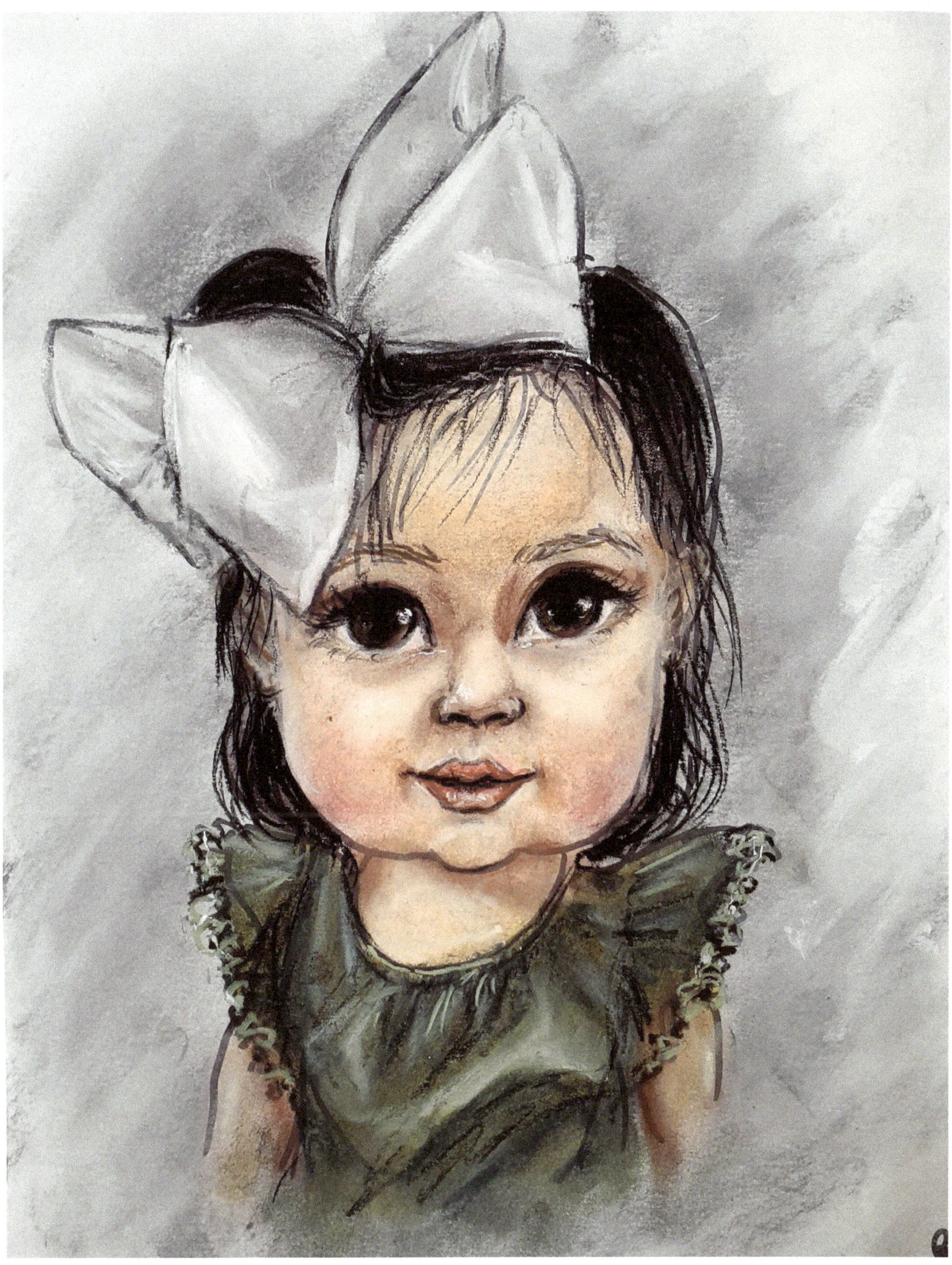

Cartoon and caricature style art may give you the freedom to let go and enjoy the process. It is satisfying to create something funny and cute.

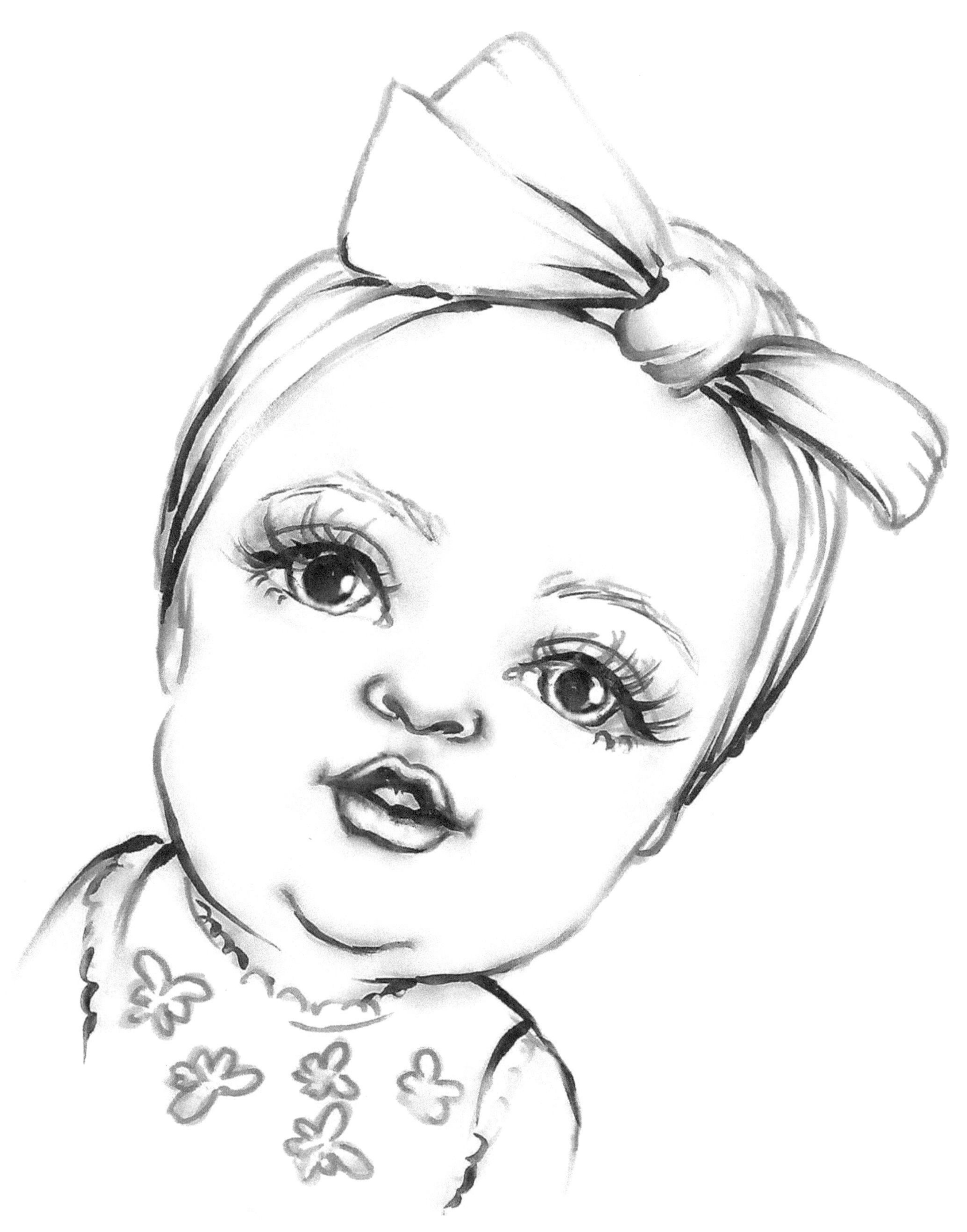

Color

Trace

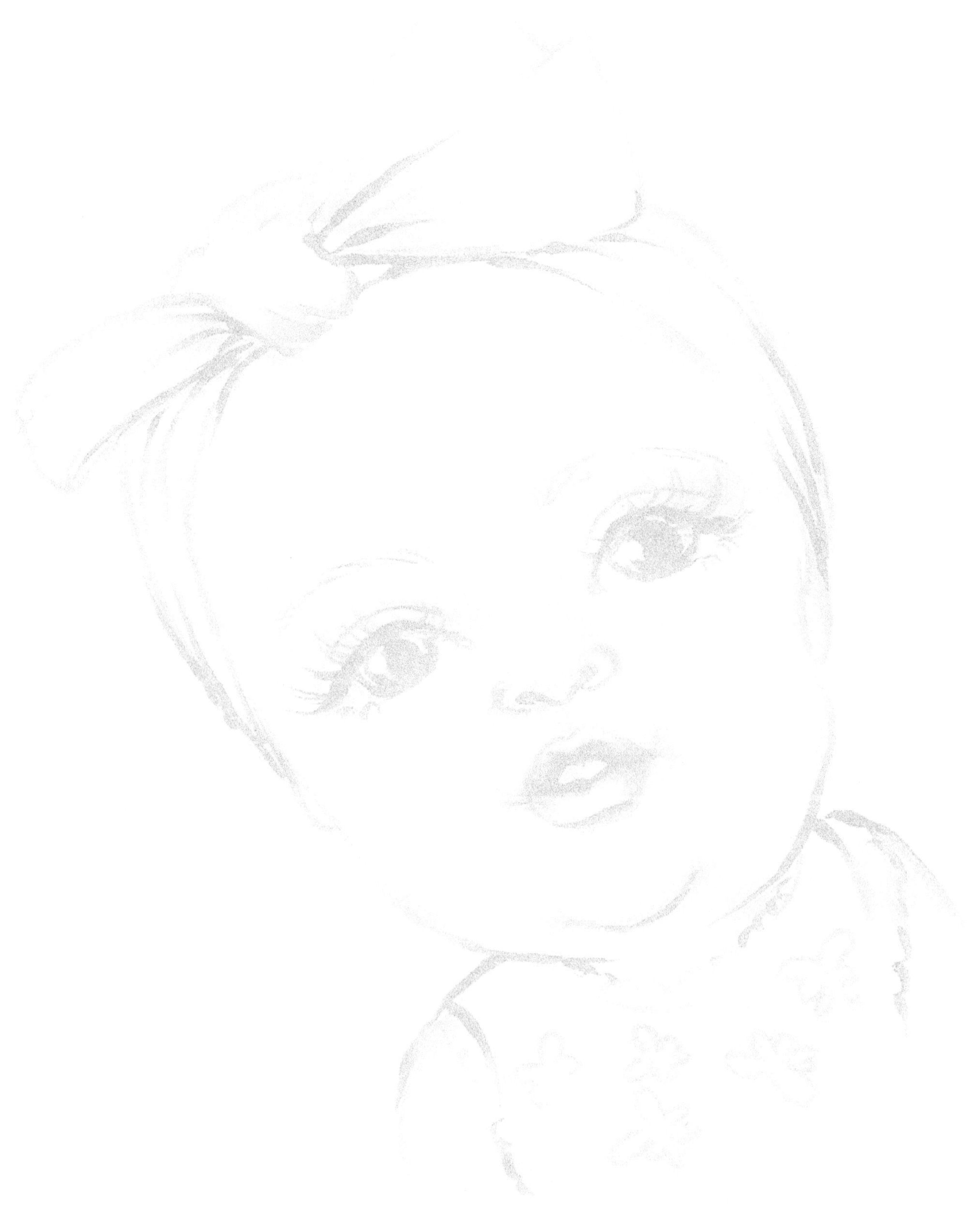

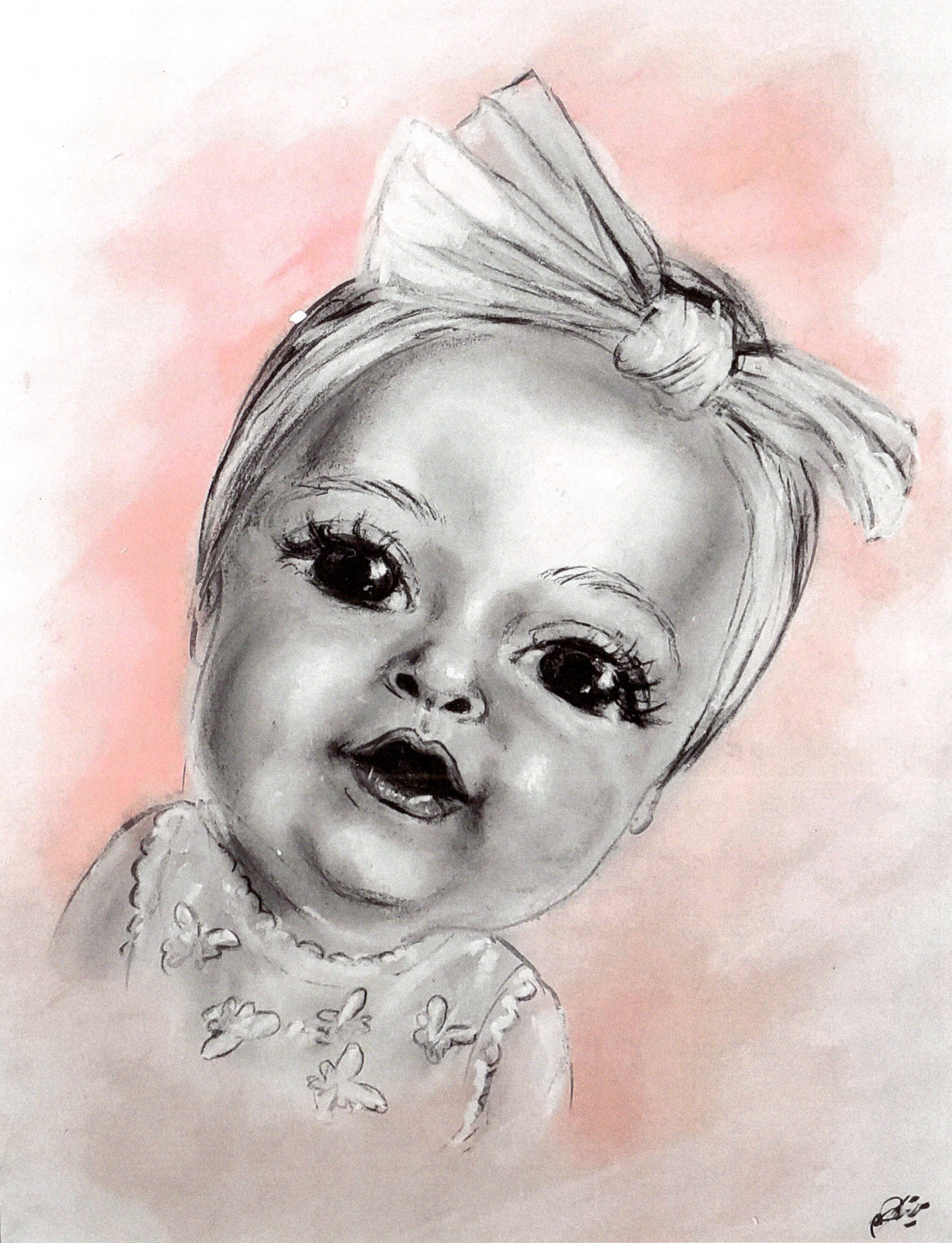

Coloring frequently engages the frontal lobe of
the brain. Specifically, it may encourage focus and
concentration and facilitates relaxation.

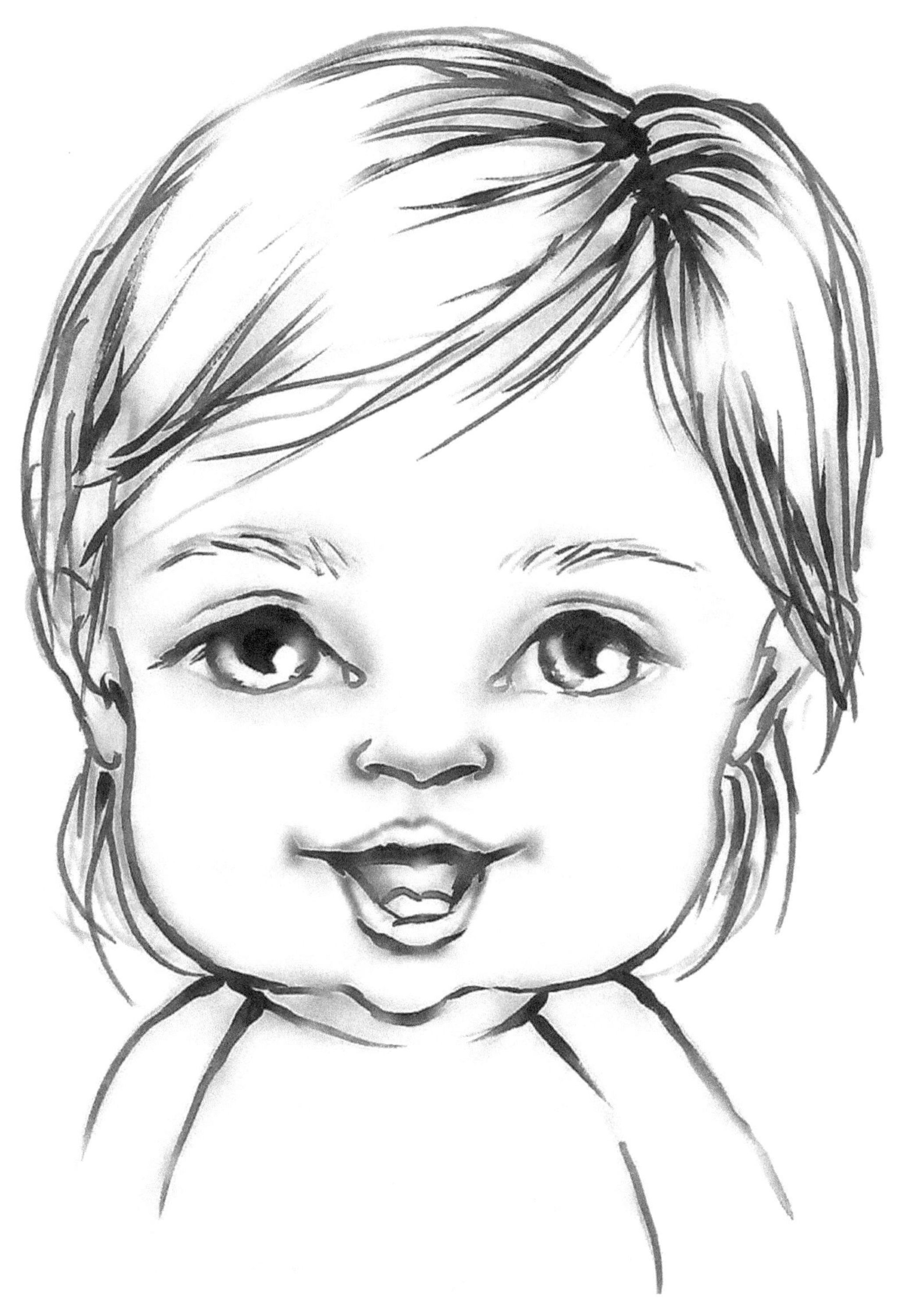

Trace

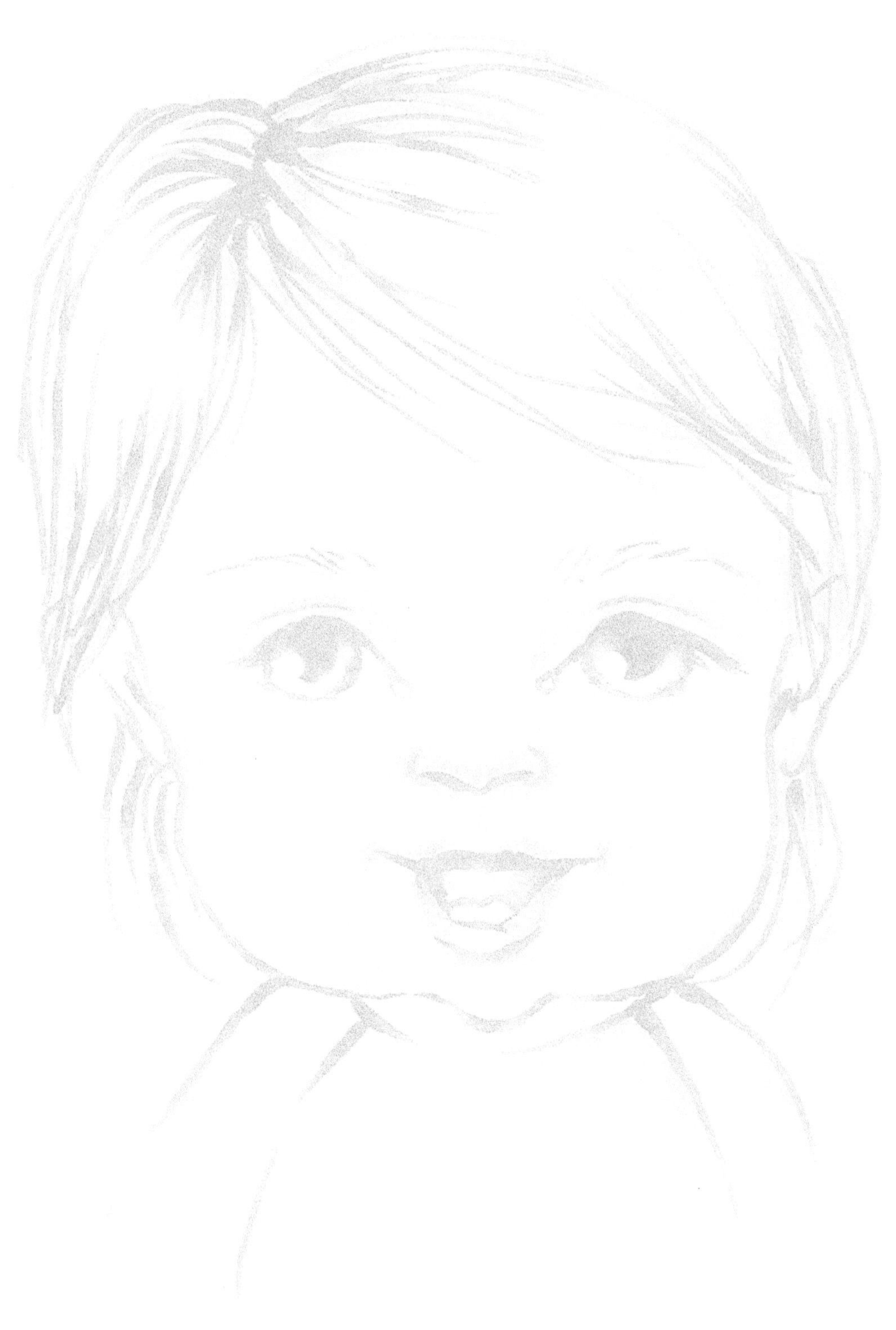

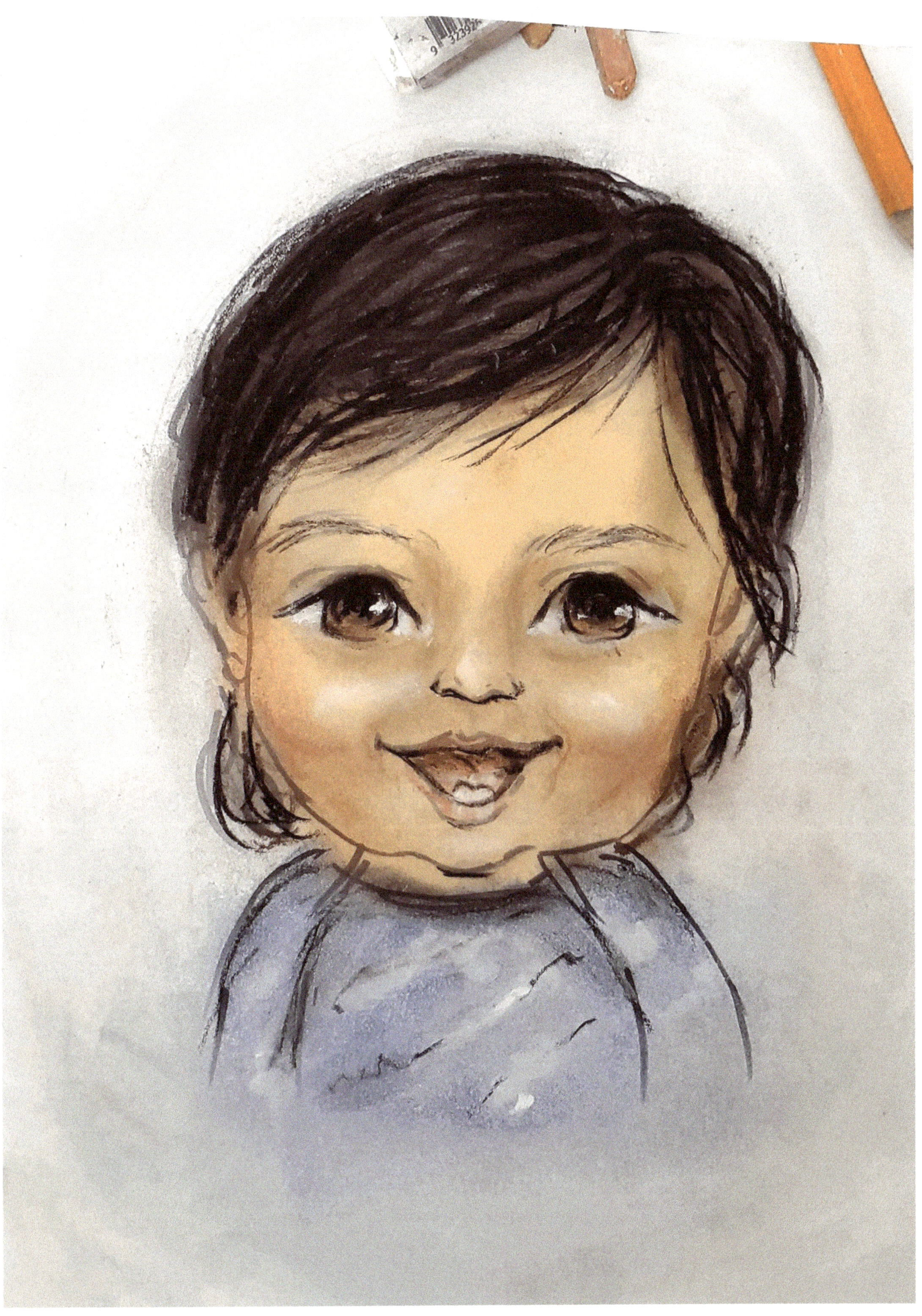

Look for the best in the people you are drawing.
Exaggerate the positive and bring joy to their lives.

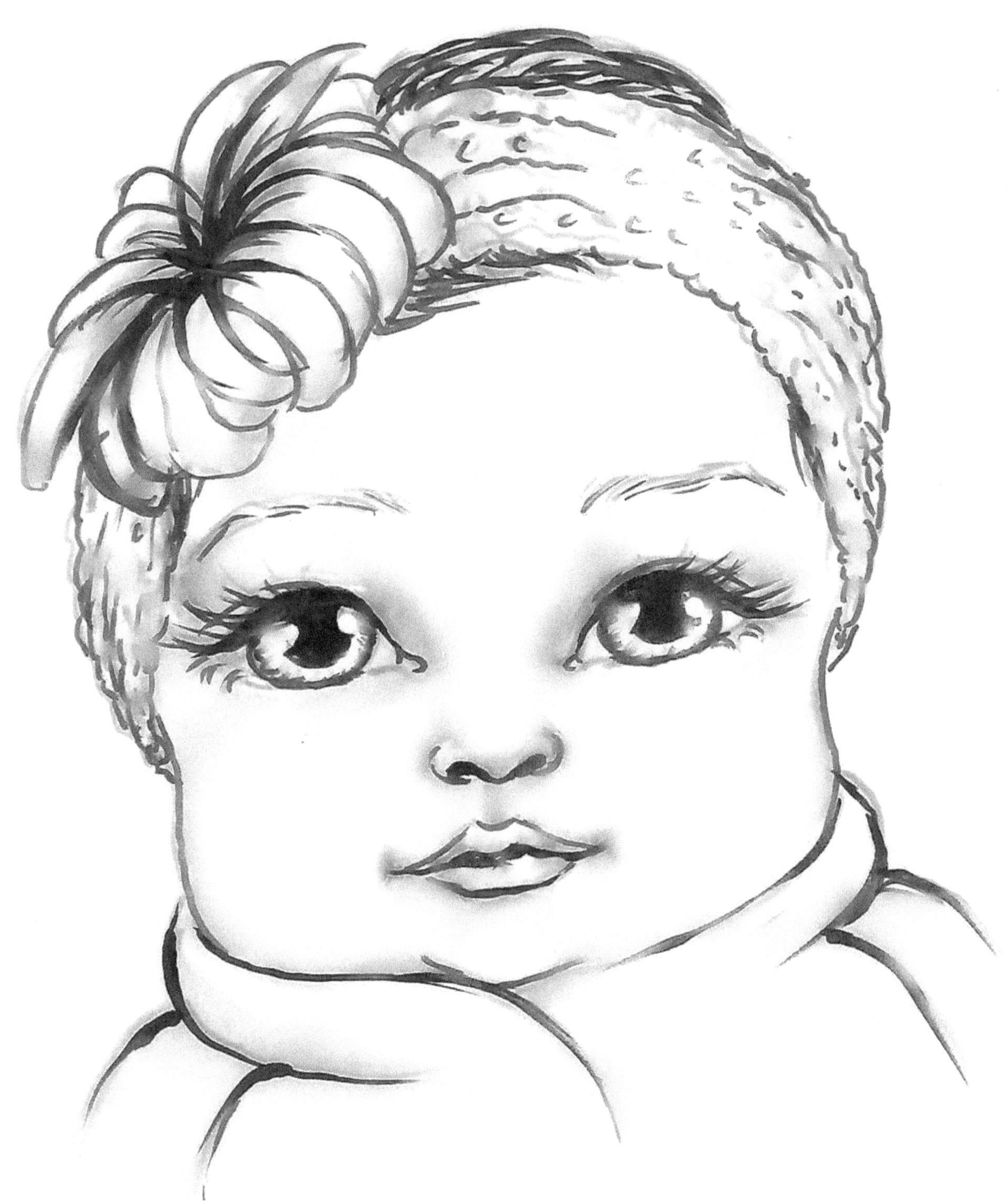

Trace

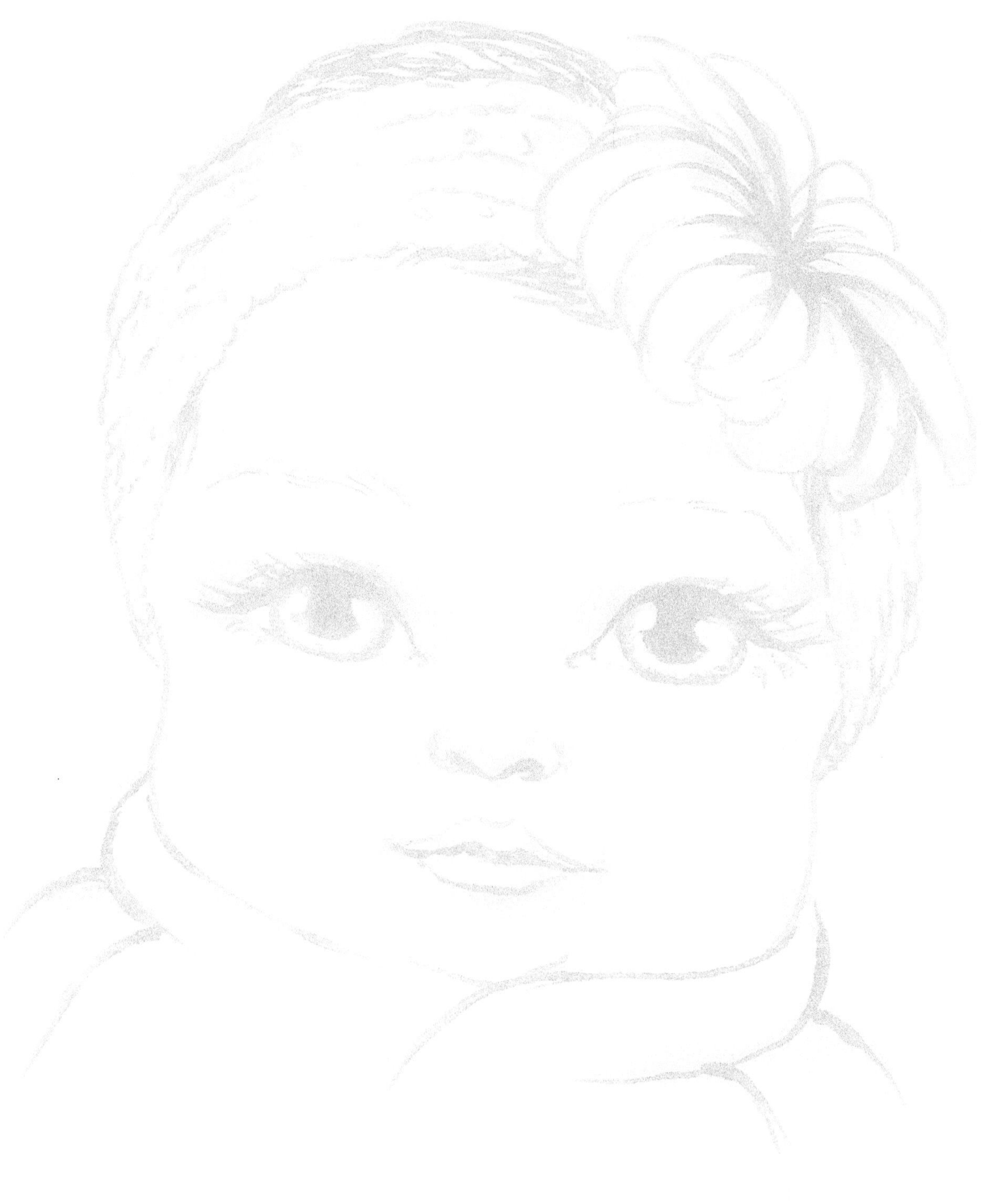

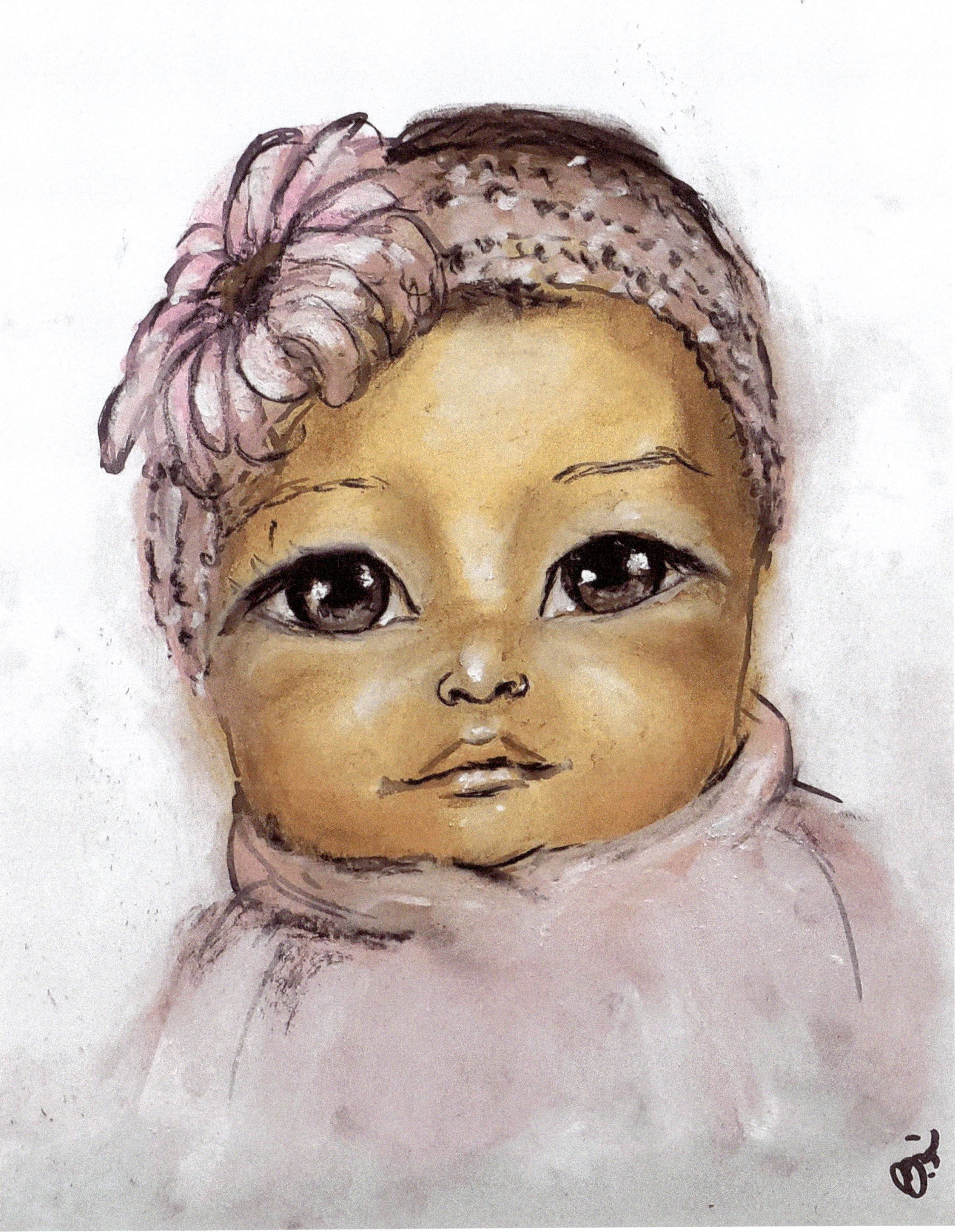

Coloring encourages relaxation. Grayscale coloring pages take the edge off coloring because some of the rendering has already been done for more three-dimensional effects.

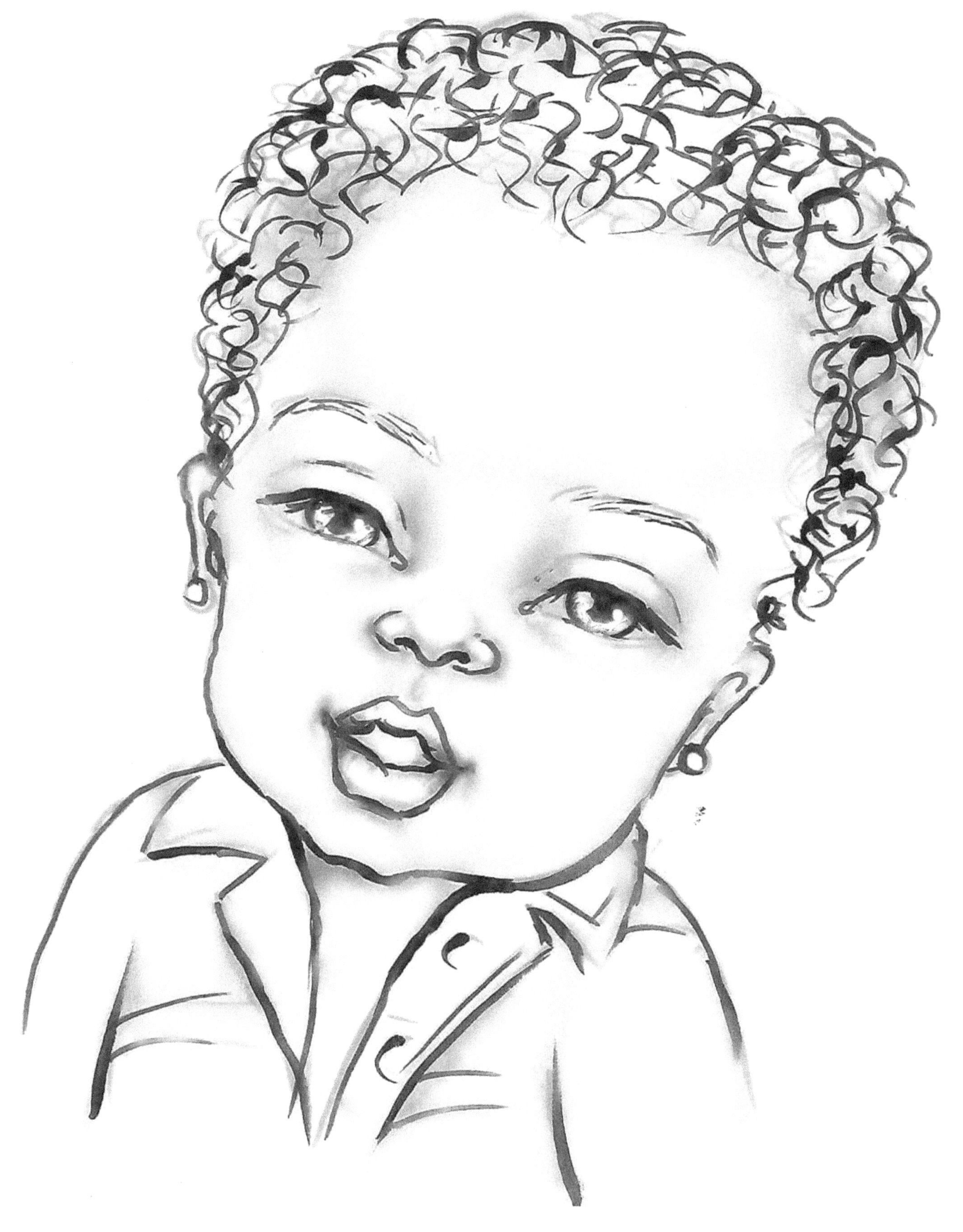

Trace

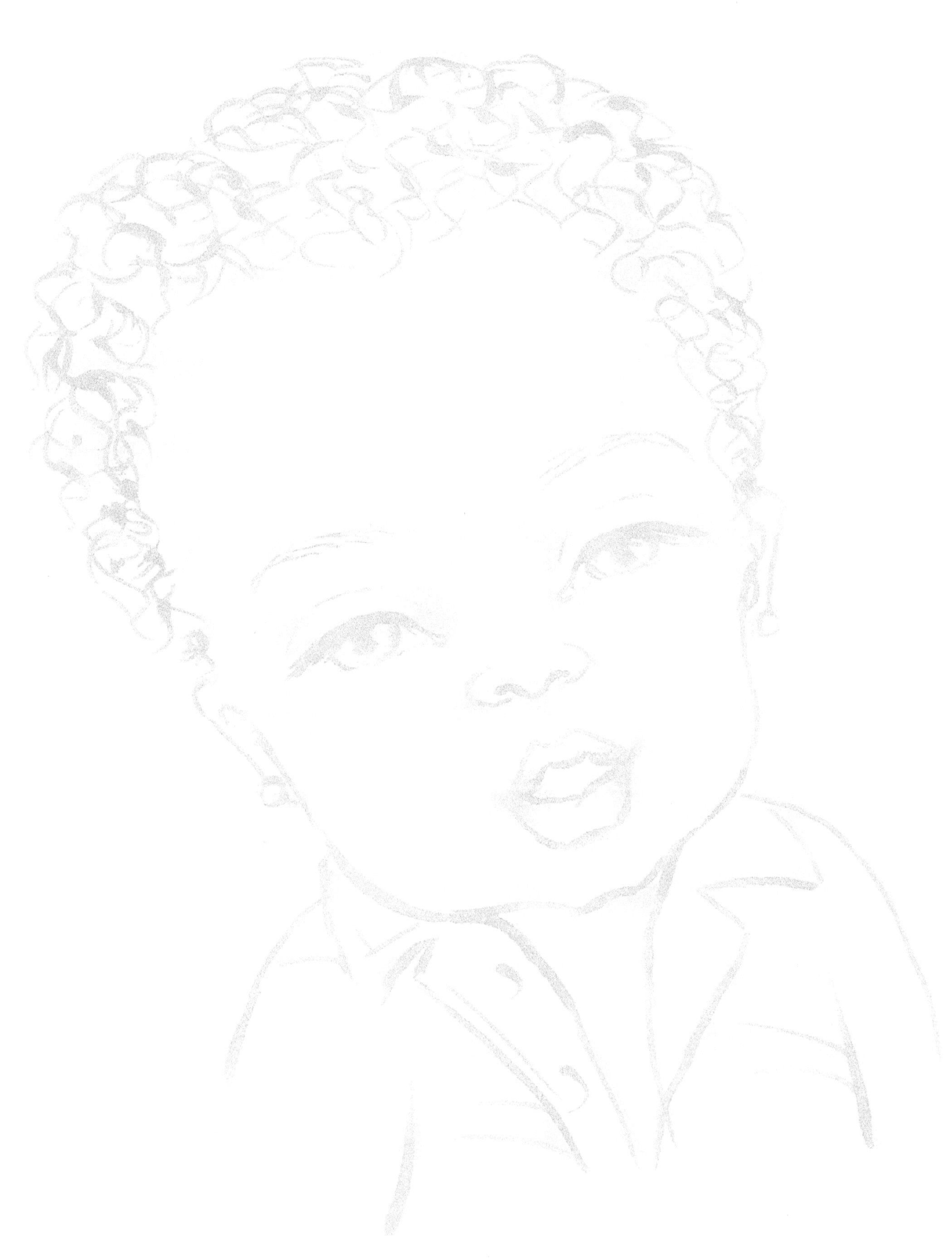

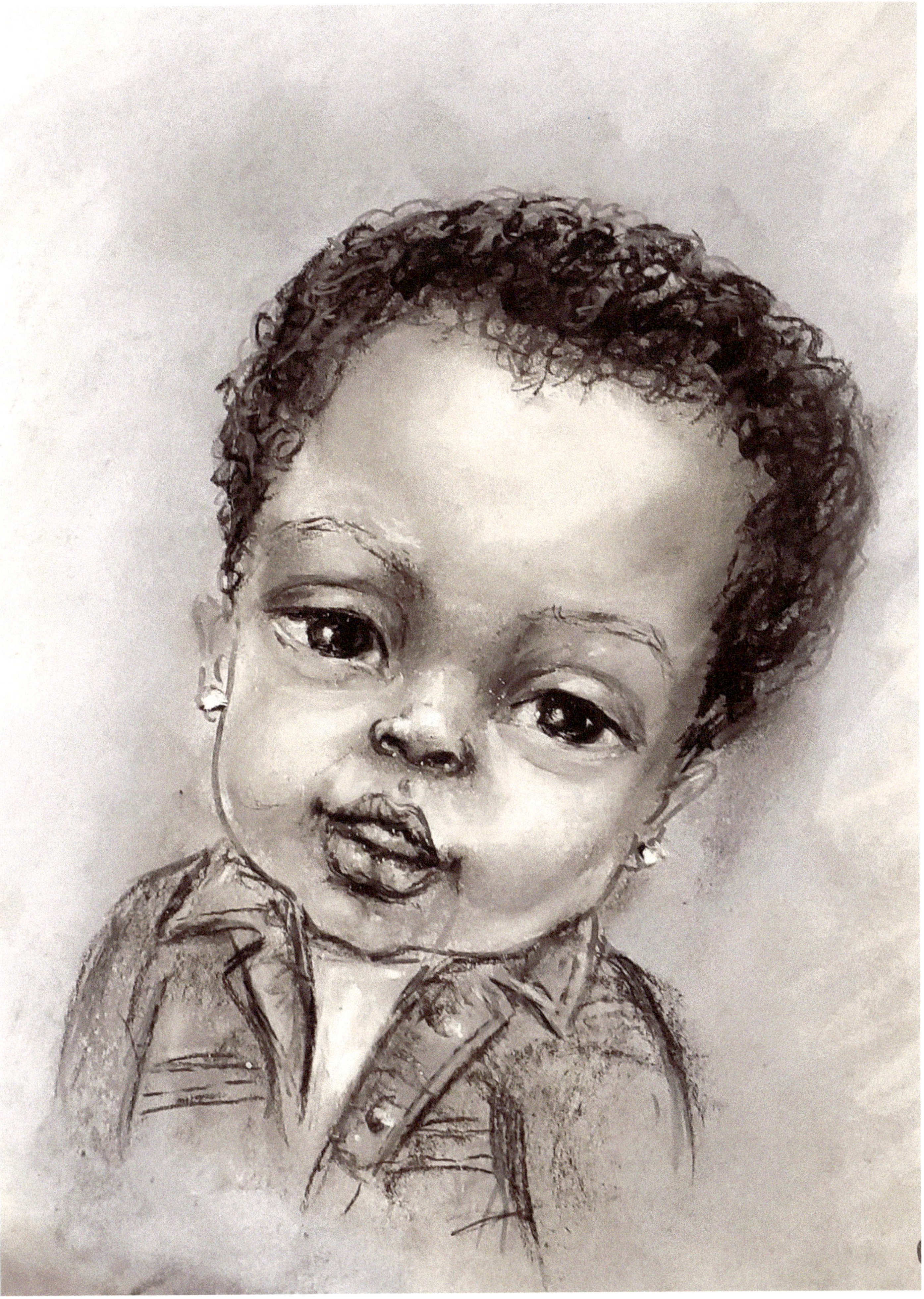

Begin your work with a prayer, thanking God for your wonderful abilities. At work, I aim to bring joy to the people I am drawing.

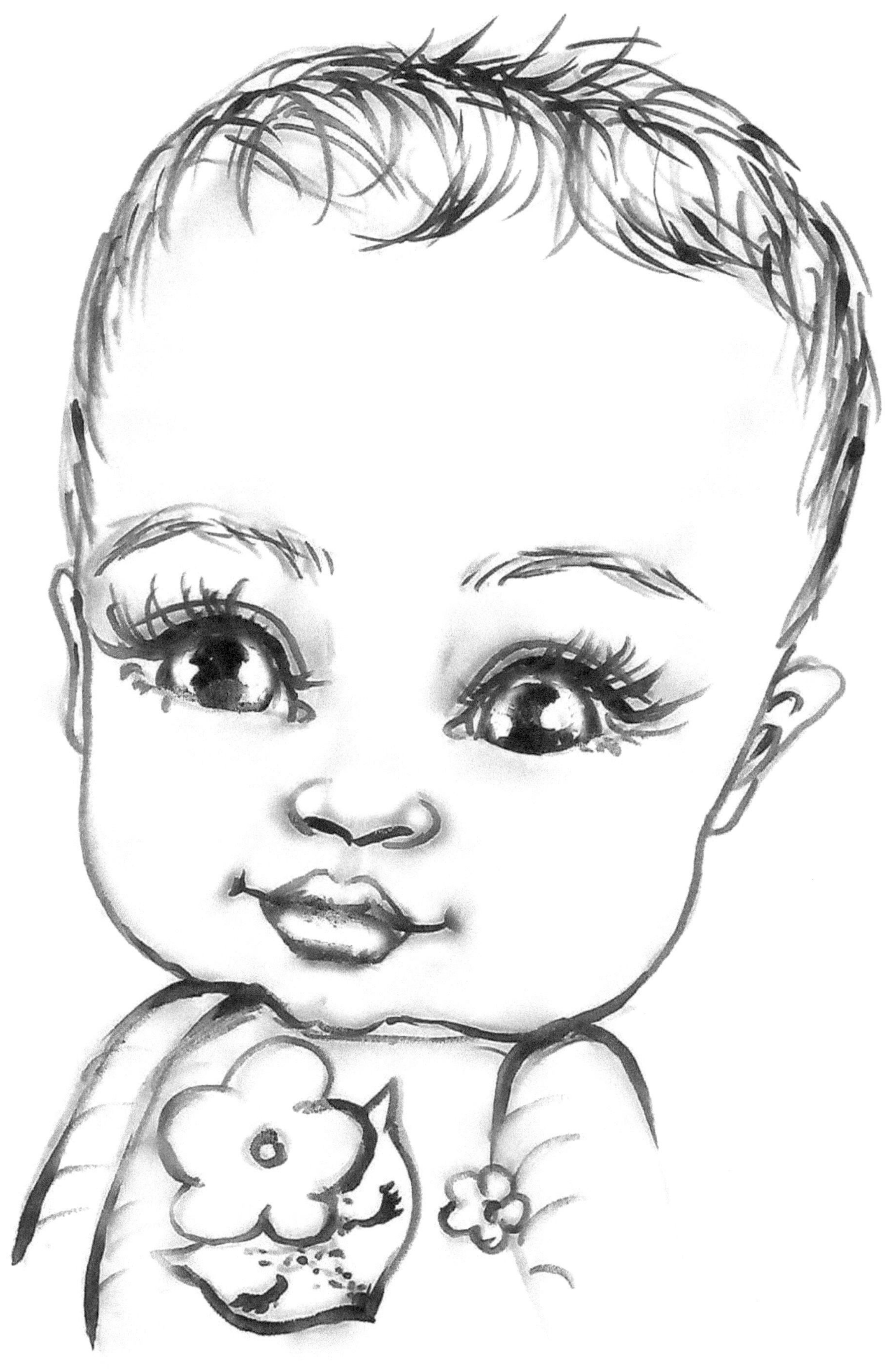
Color

Trace

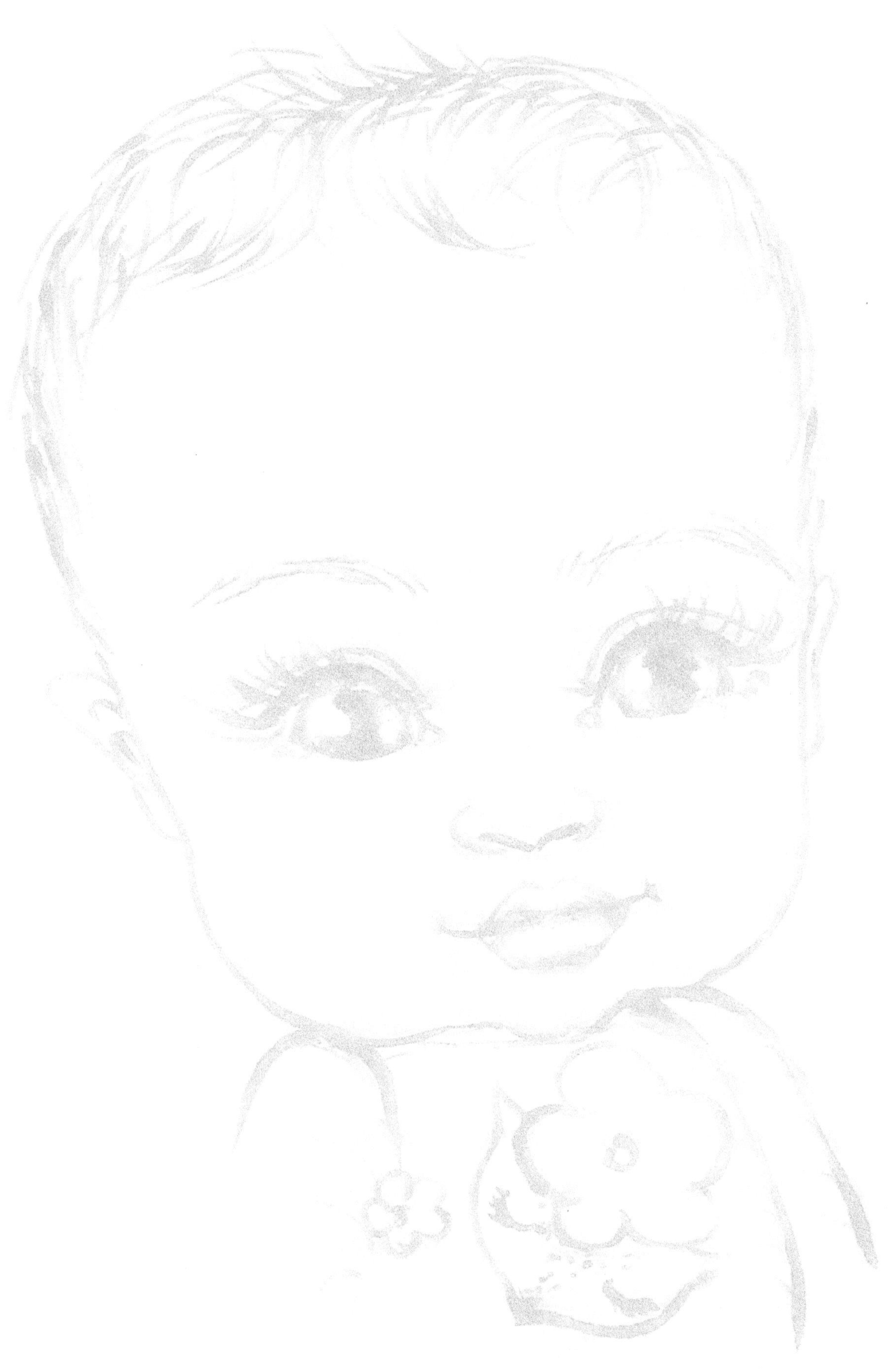

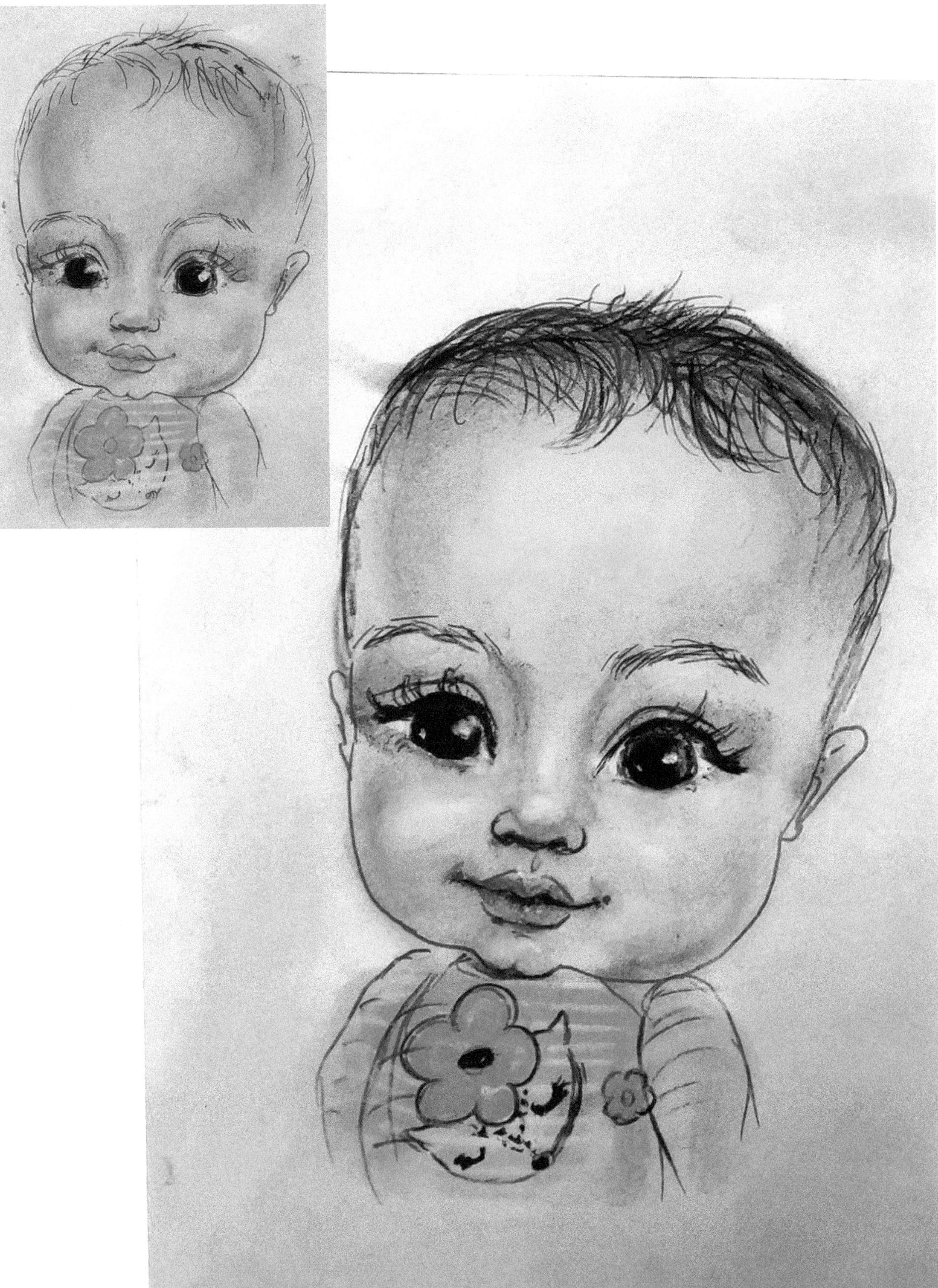

As you color babies try to think about happy memories
from your childhood. Try to think about the time you
were a baby.

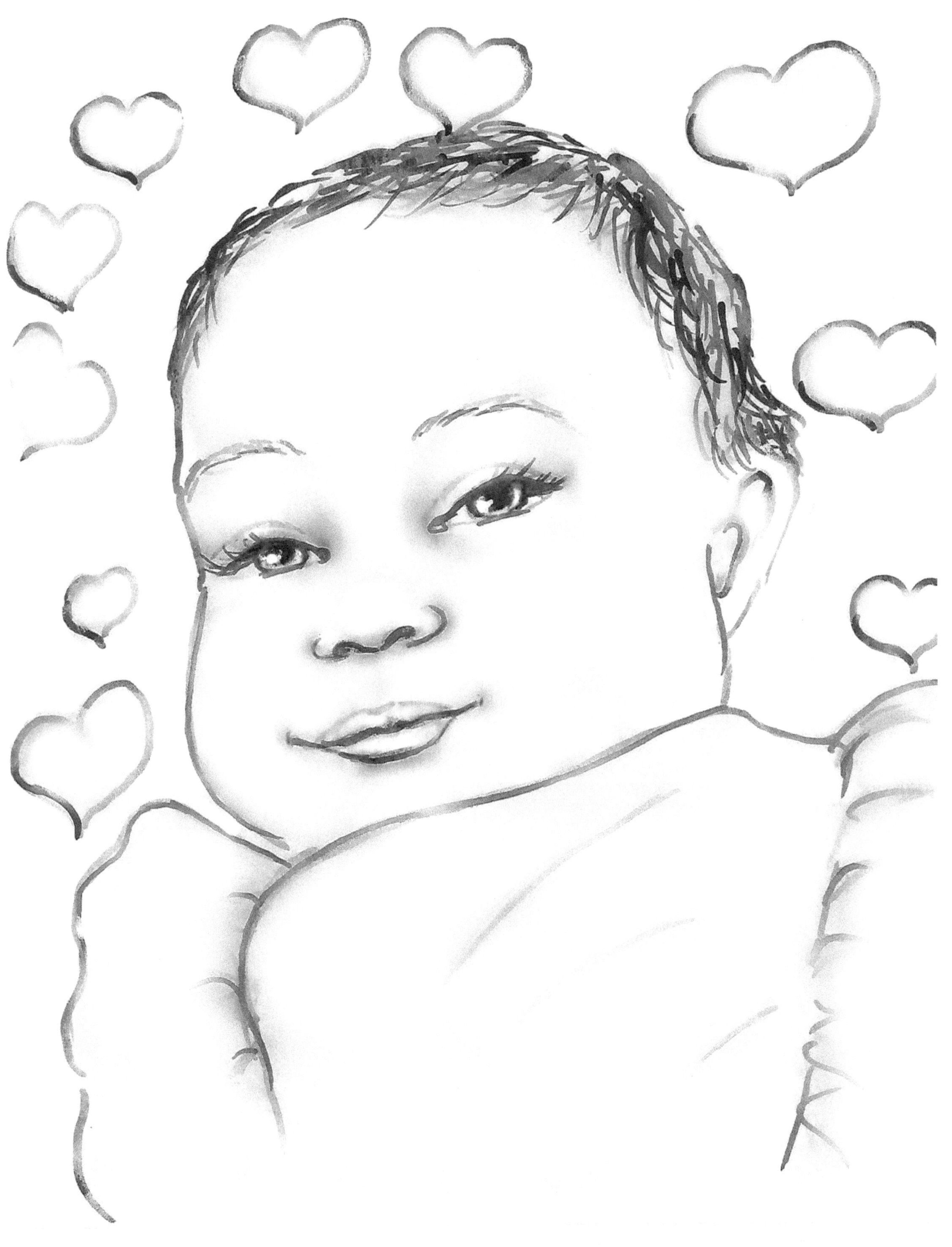
Color

Trace

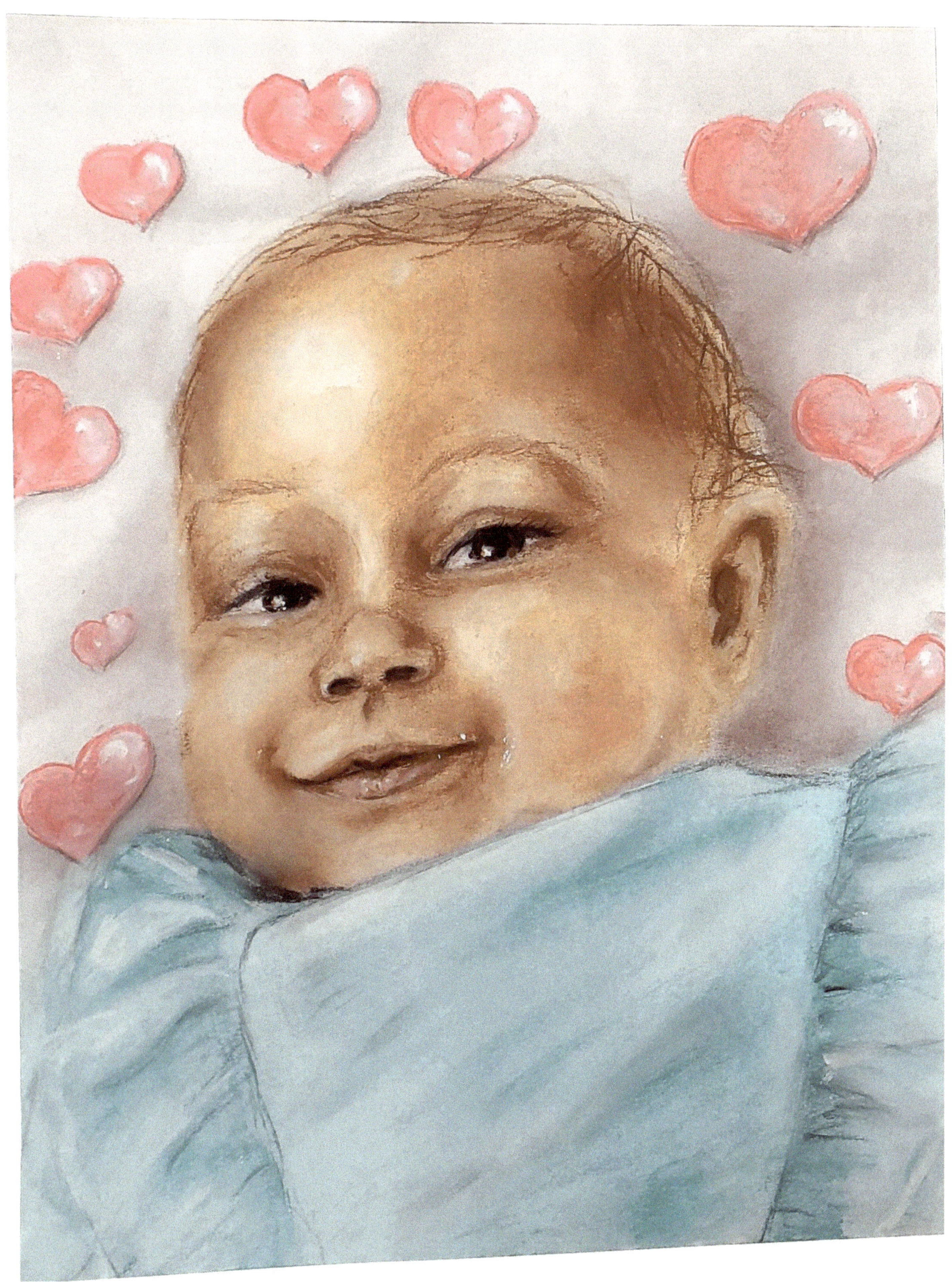

Think about babies cooing, and laughing. Replace any
negative thoughts with positive and pleasant ones.

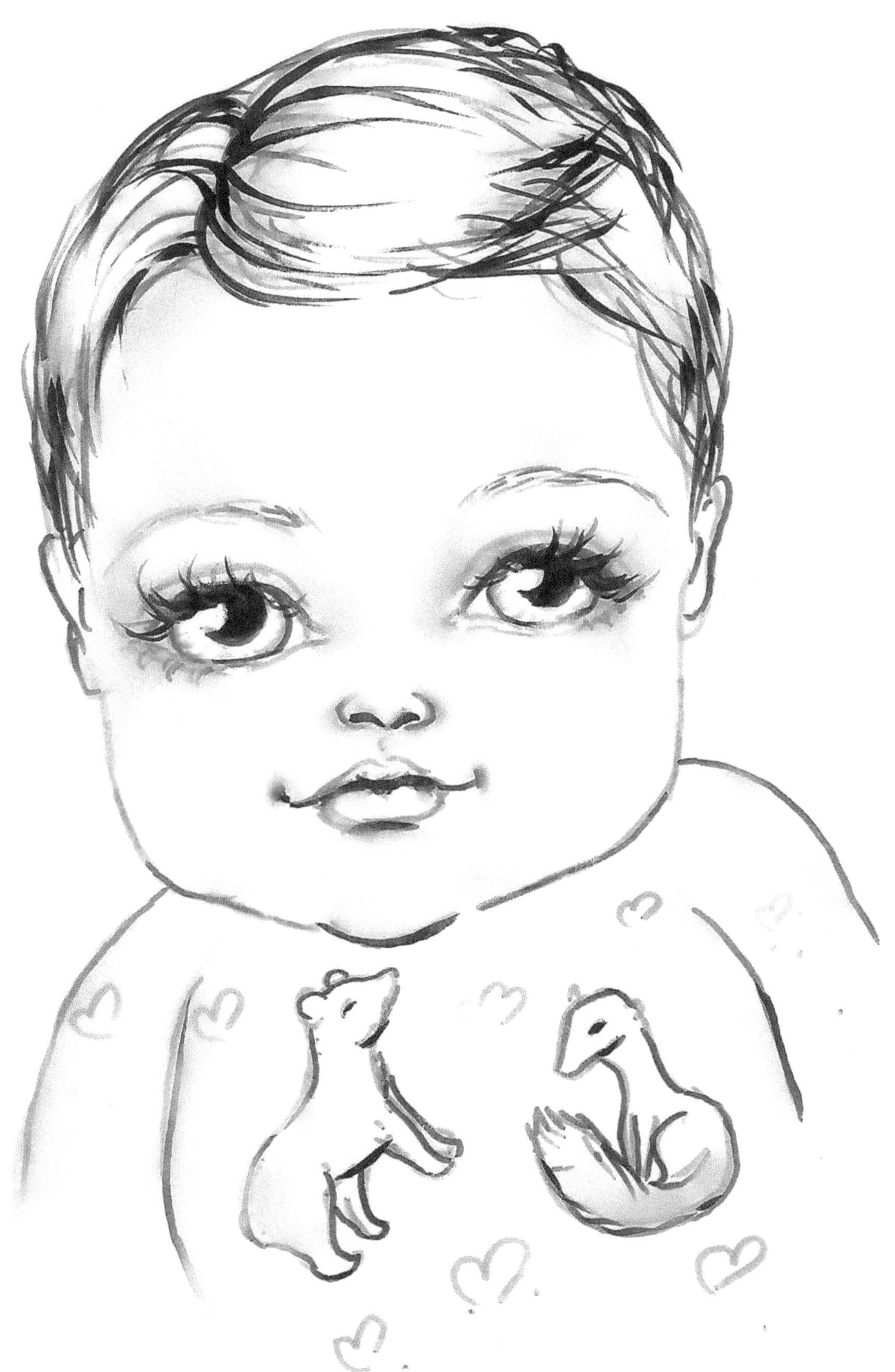

Trace

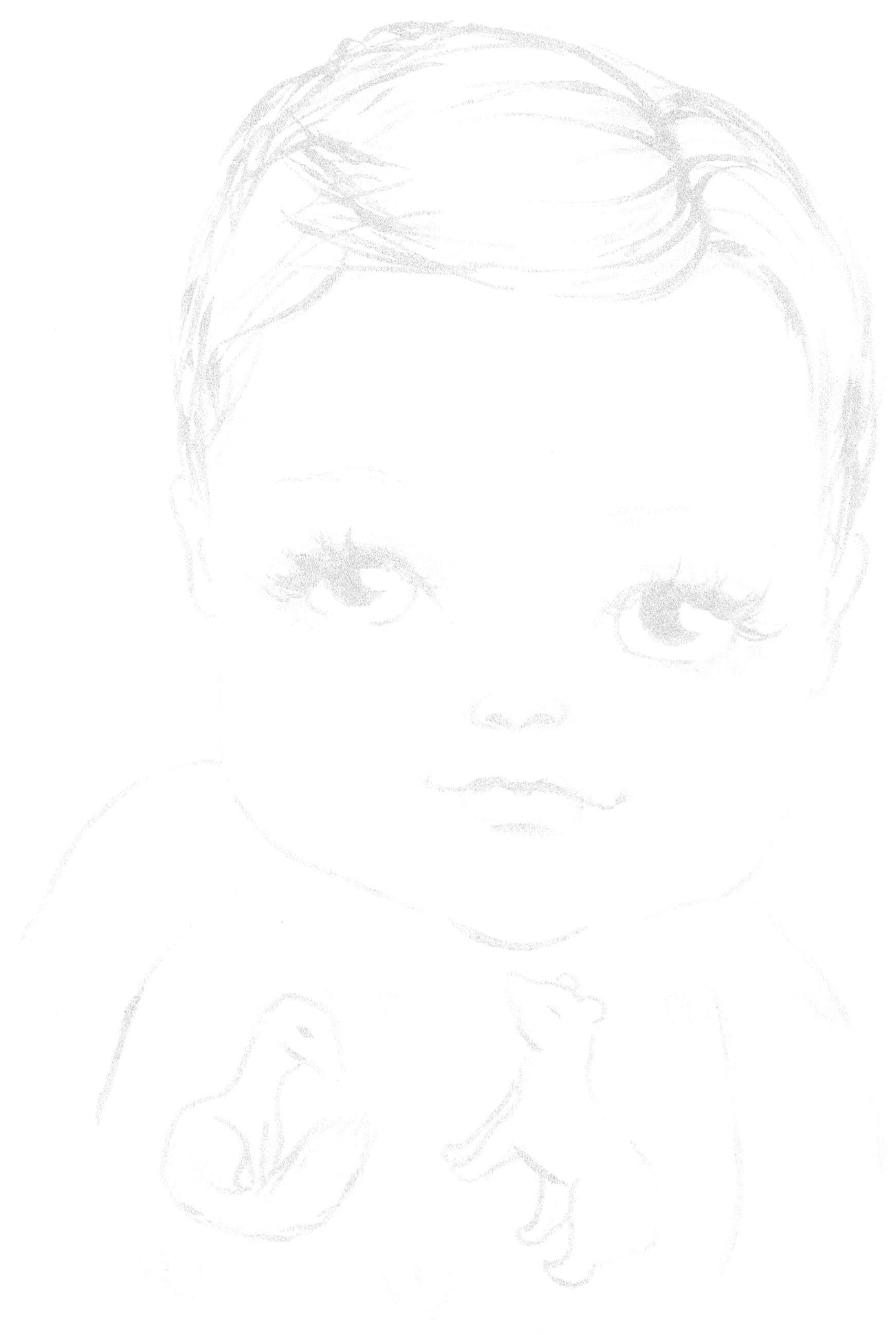

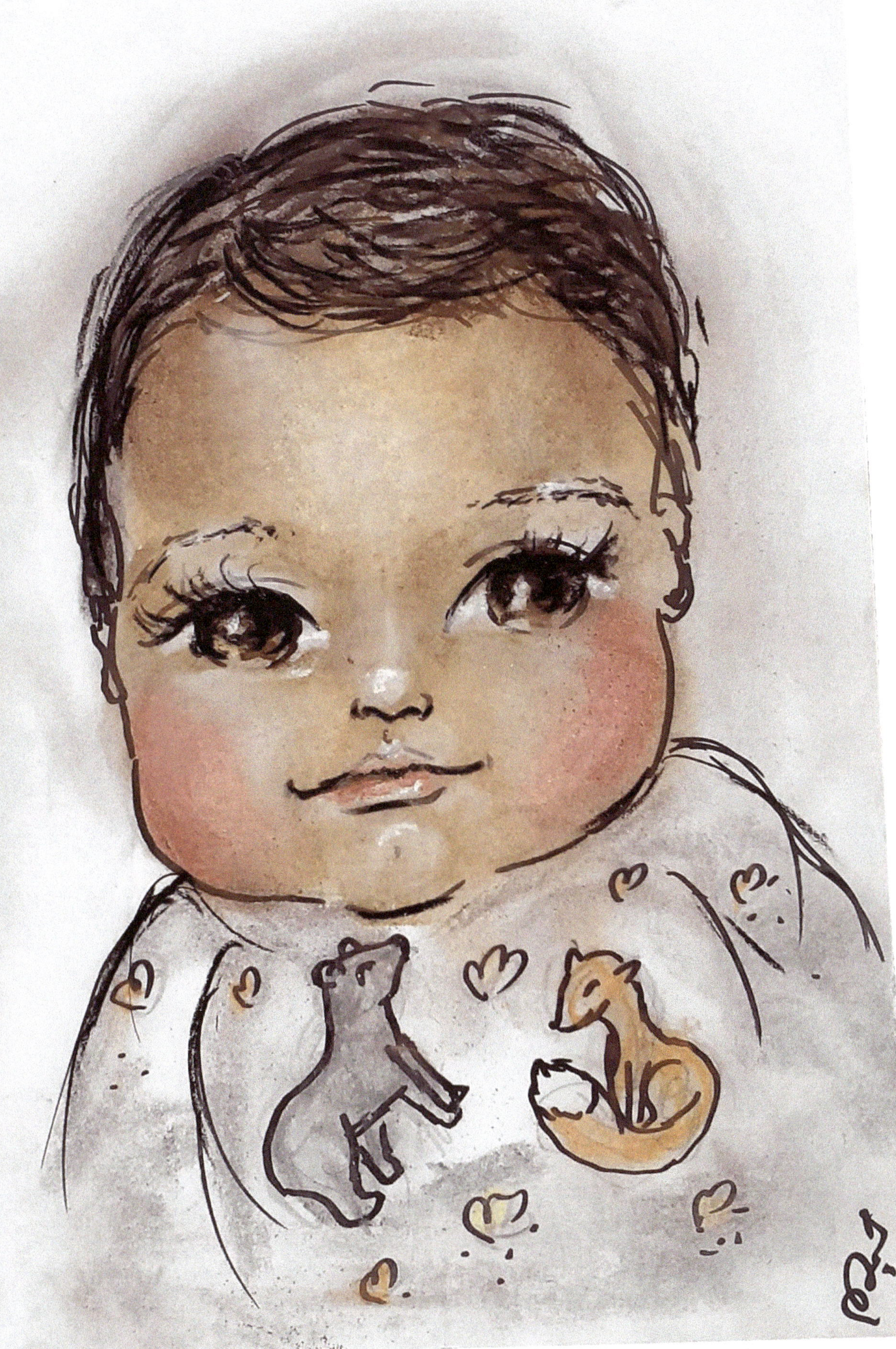

Studying different facial expressions and emotions is a step toward character creation and animation. However, in live caricature drawing and portrait commissions, most of the faces you'll be drawing will be facing forward with a smile.

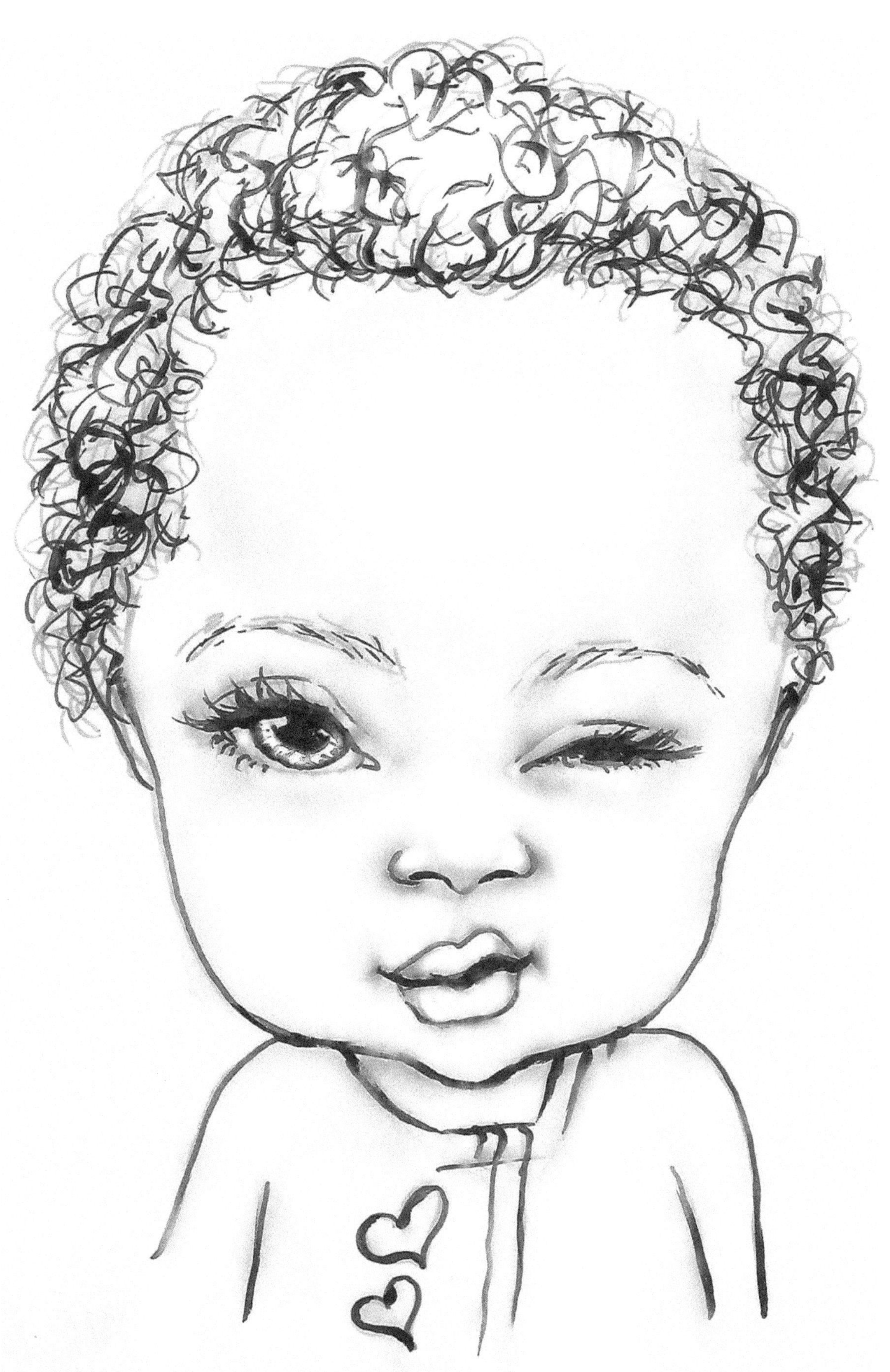

Trace

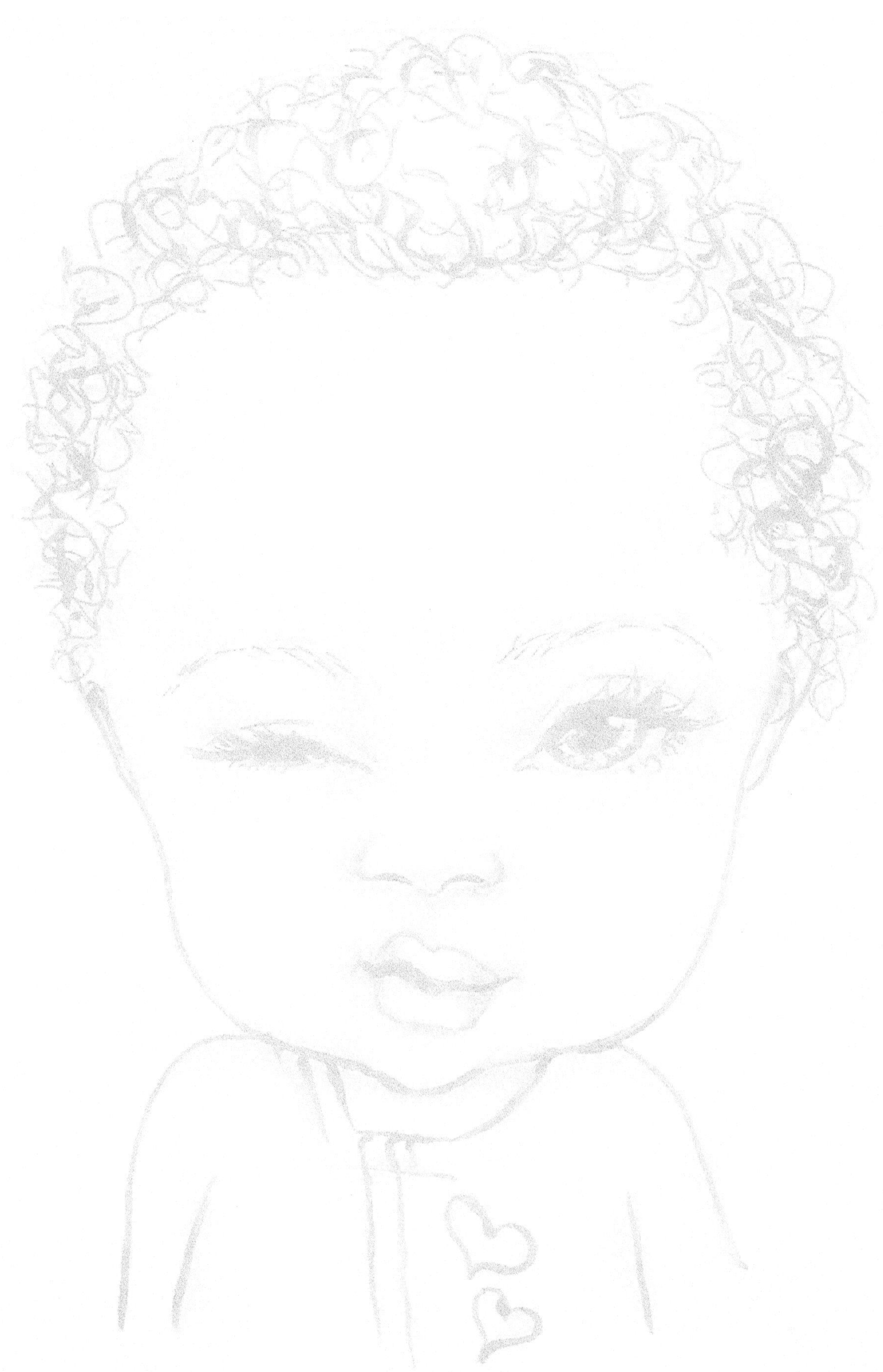

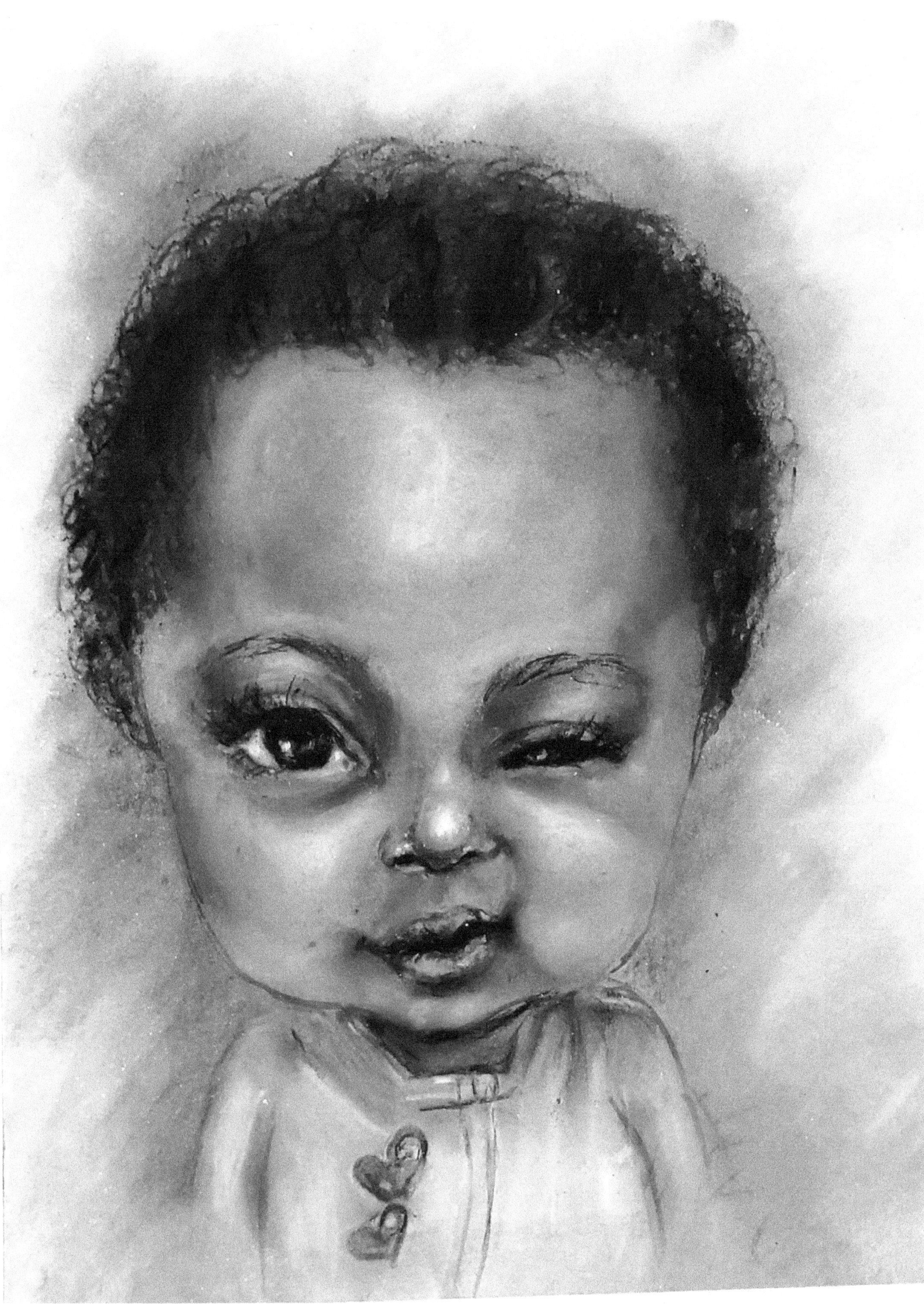

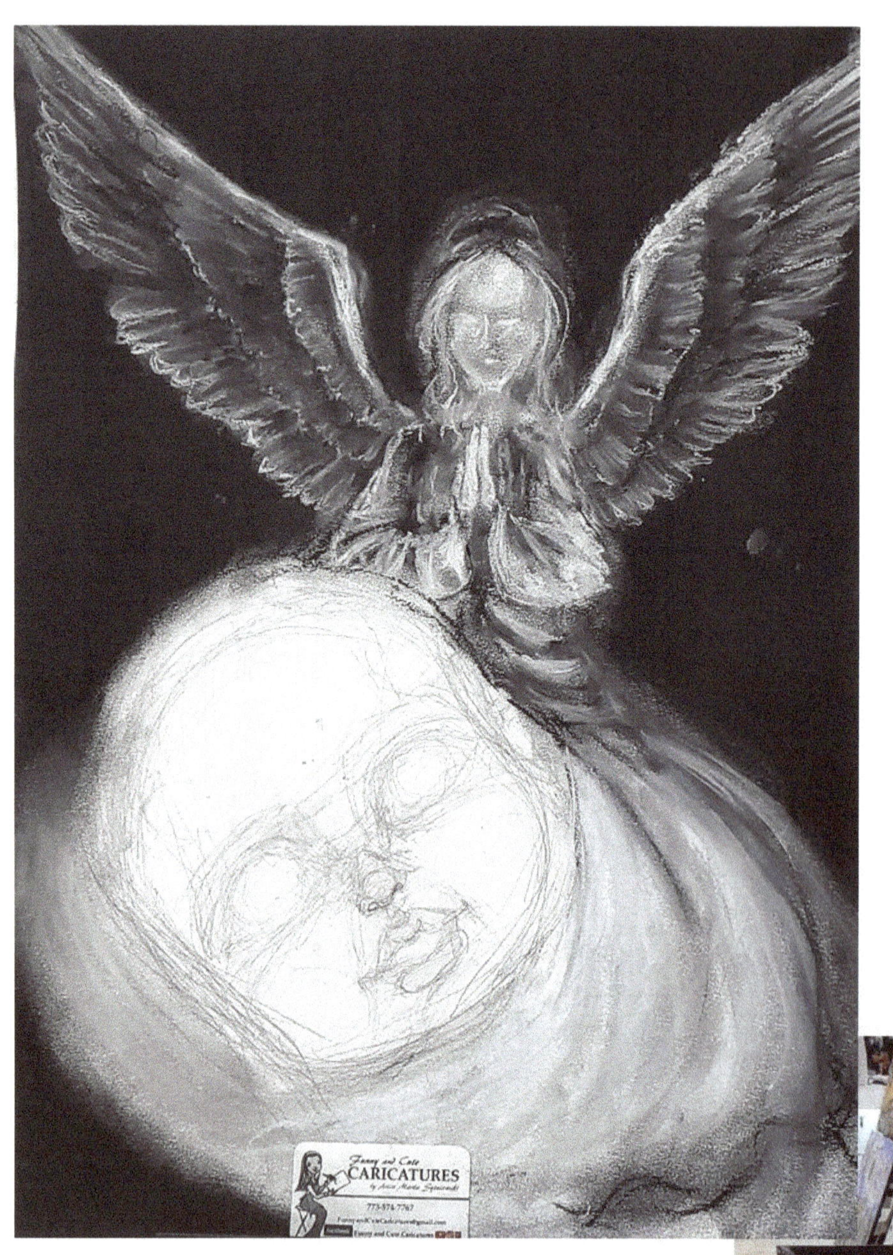

It is all **thanks to God,** and because of God, that I am able to work as an artist.

God is the true beginning and the ultimate end of any good work

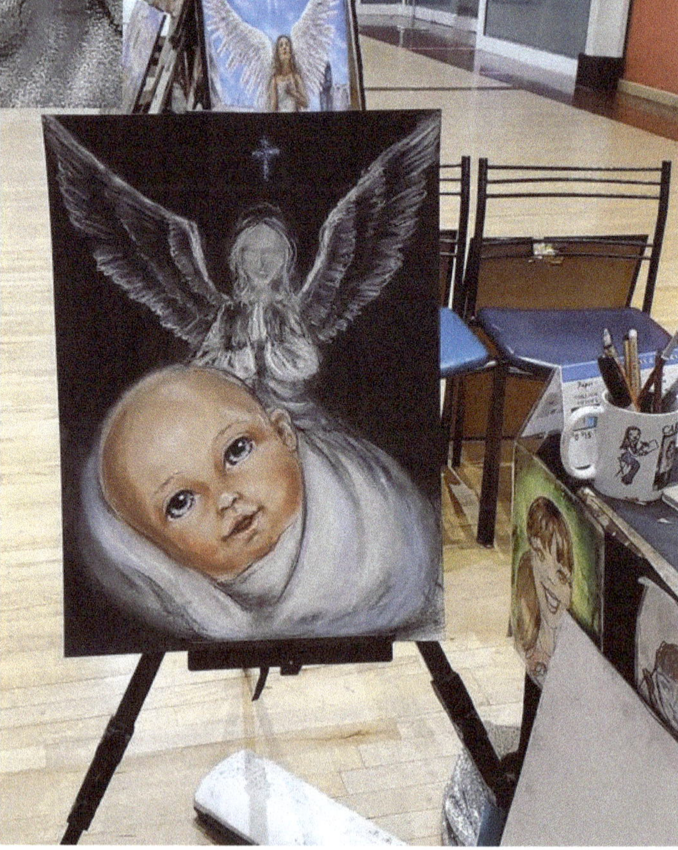

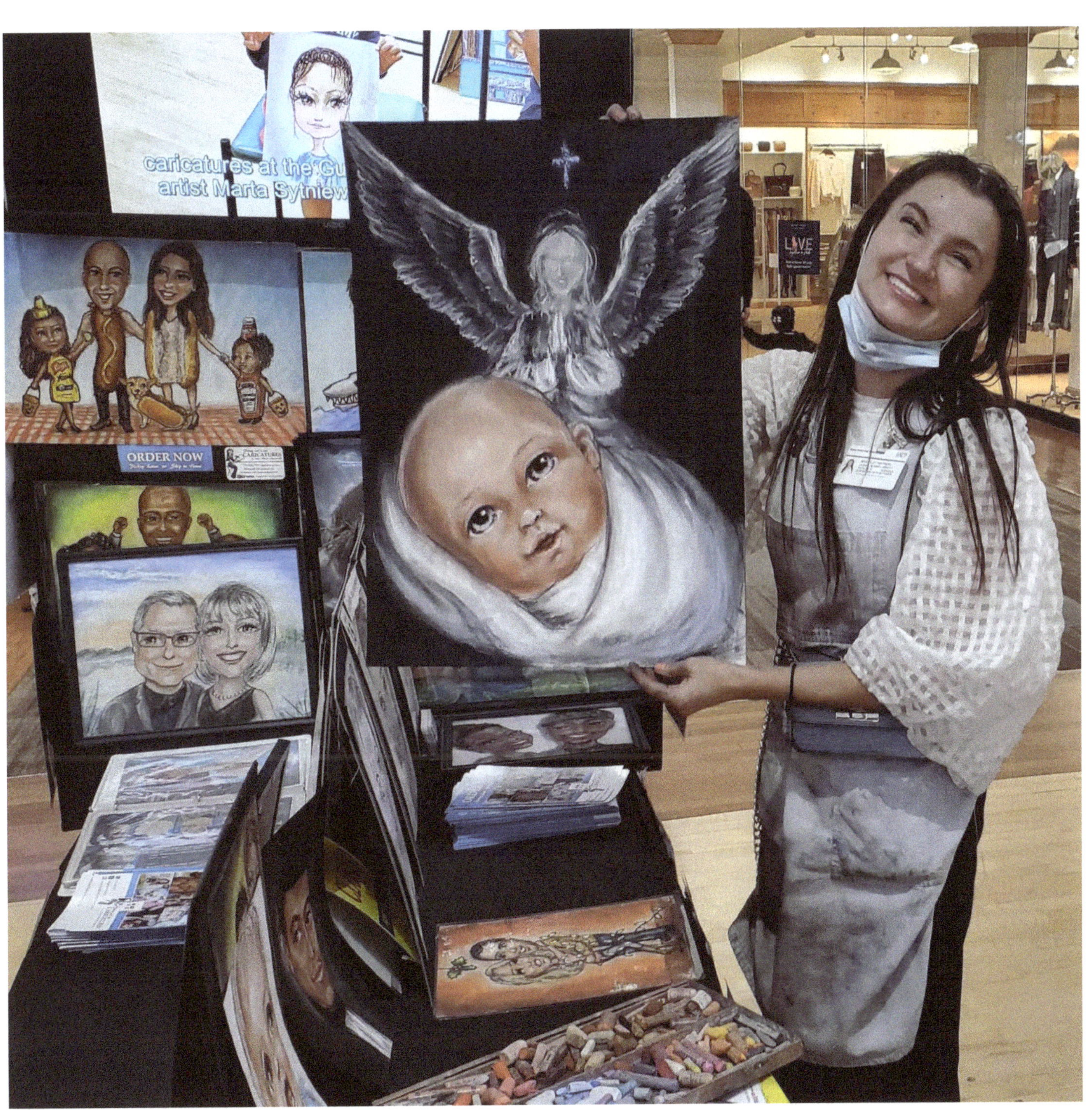

caricatures at the Gu...
artist Marta Sytniew...
ORDER NOW
CARICATURES
LIVE

Through art, you can make manifest spiritual truth.
Clients often ask me to draw someone with angels, Jesus, and the Virgin Mary.

Baby portrait and caricature art is a thoughtful gift for a baby's baptism, for expecting
parents and new parents, for grandparents, and the baby's birthday.

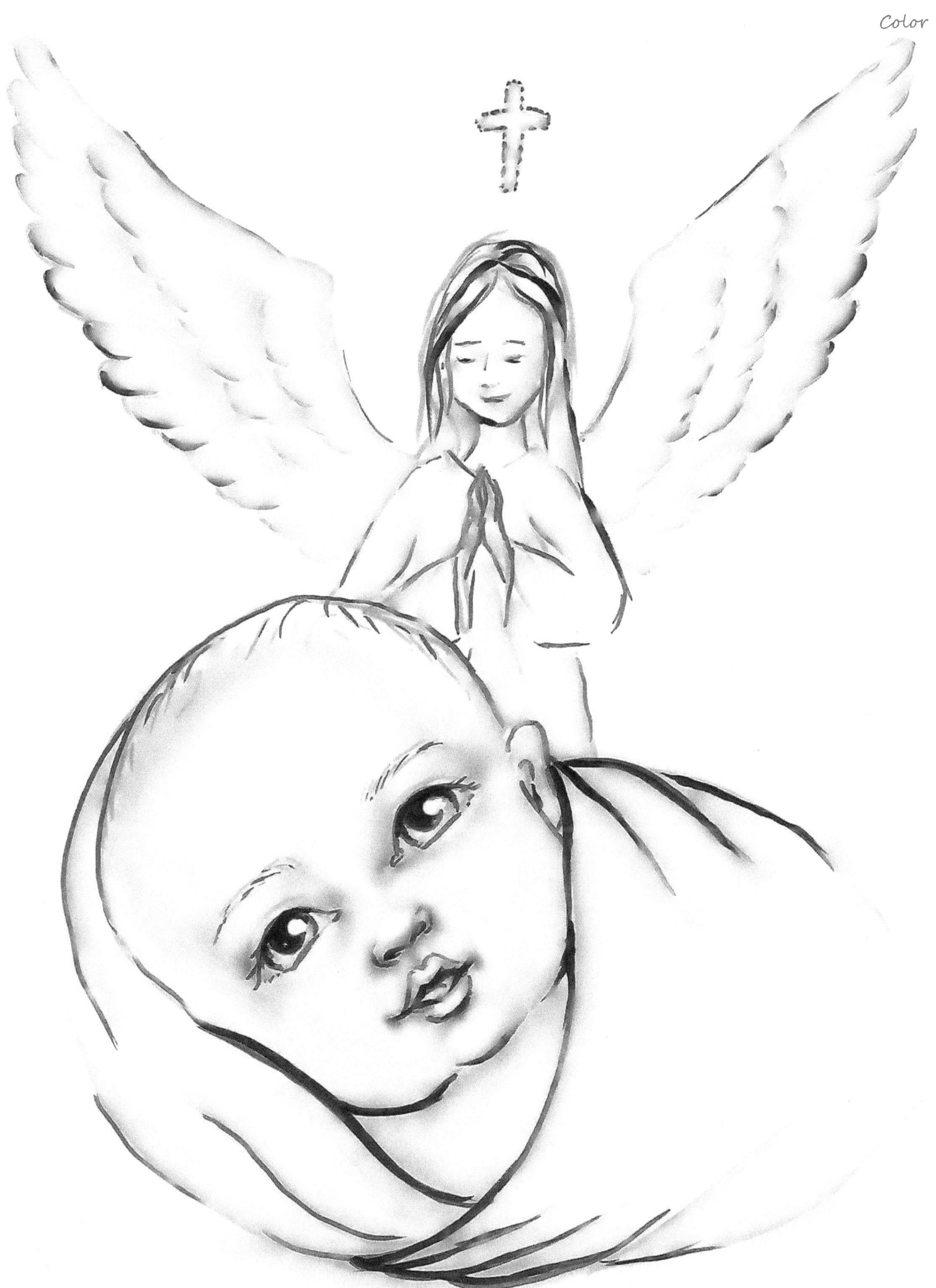
Color

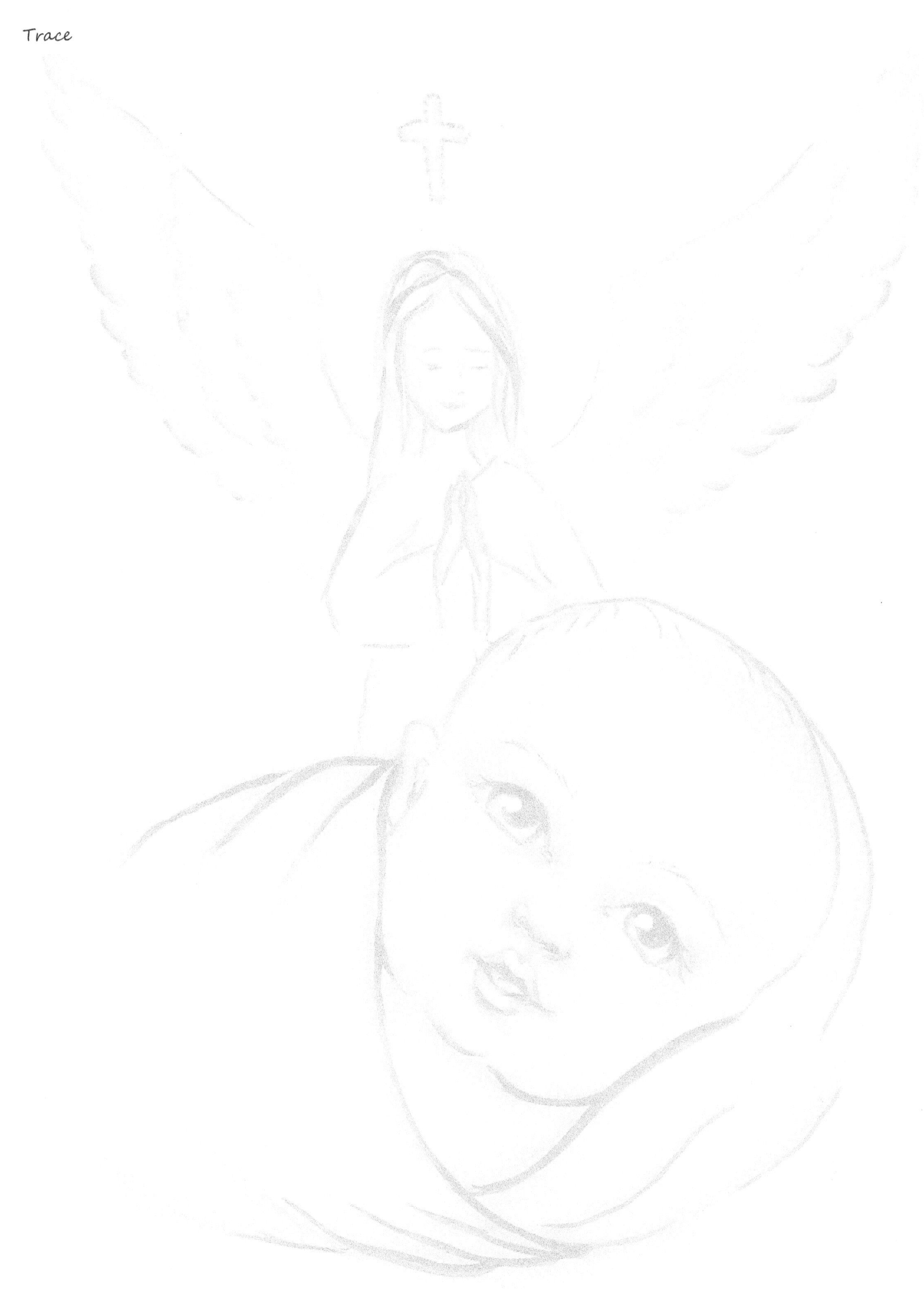
Trace

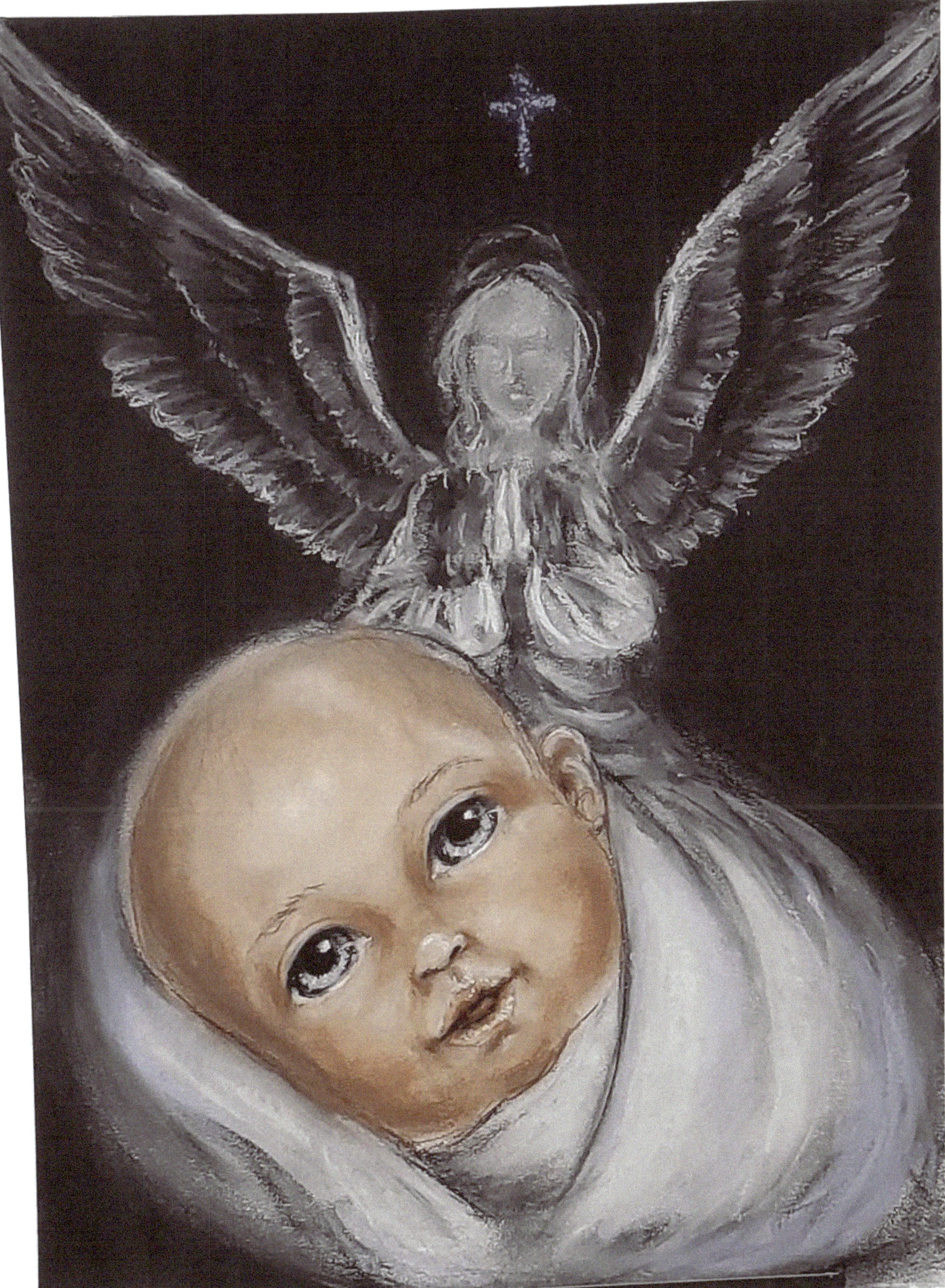

Try drawing the children you love with hearts, flowers and stars in the background. It is fun and cute .

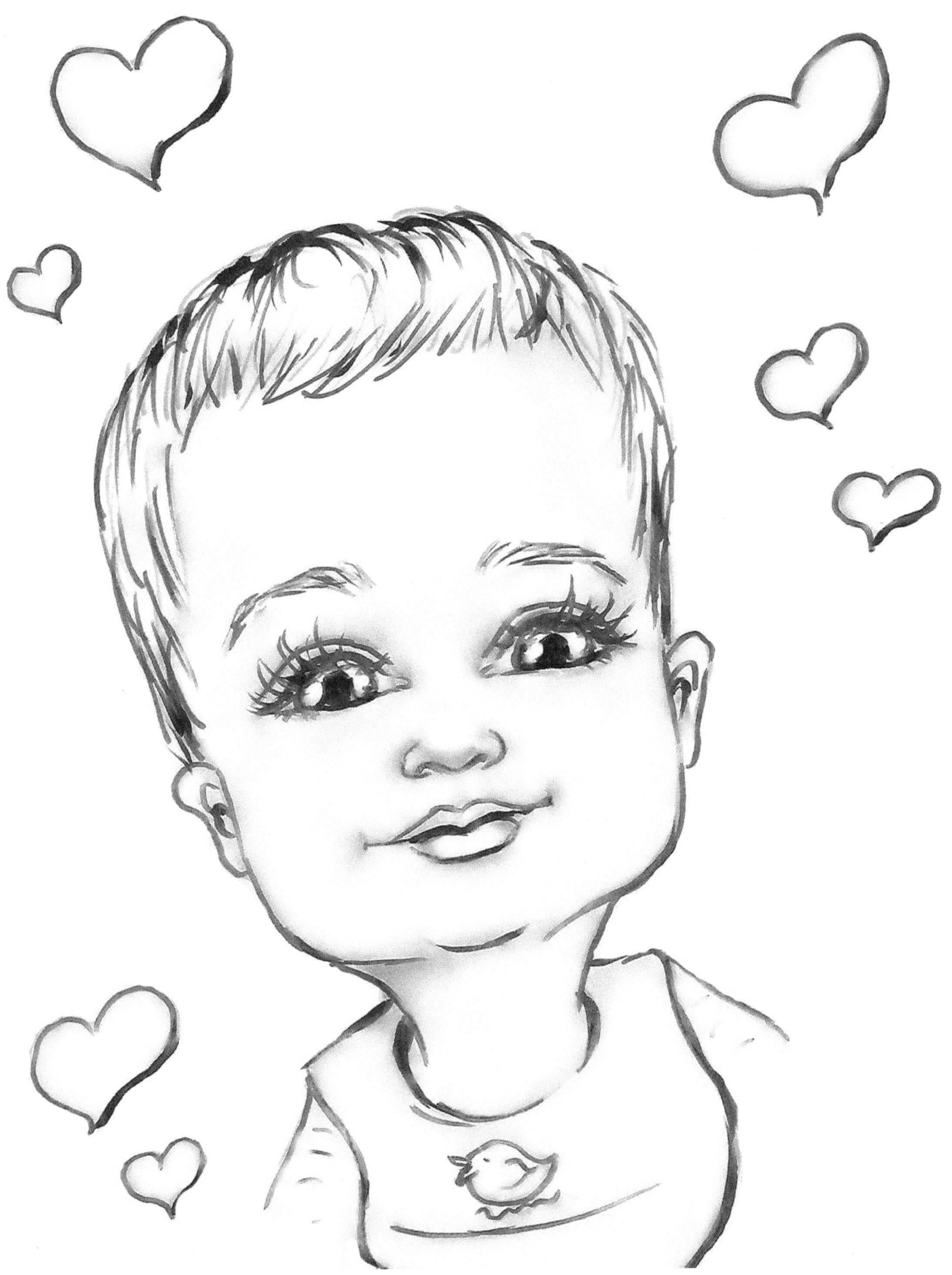

Trace

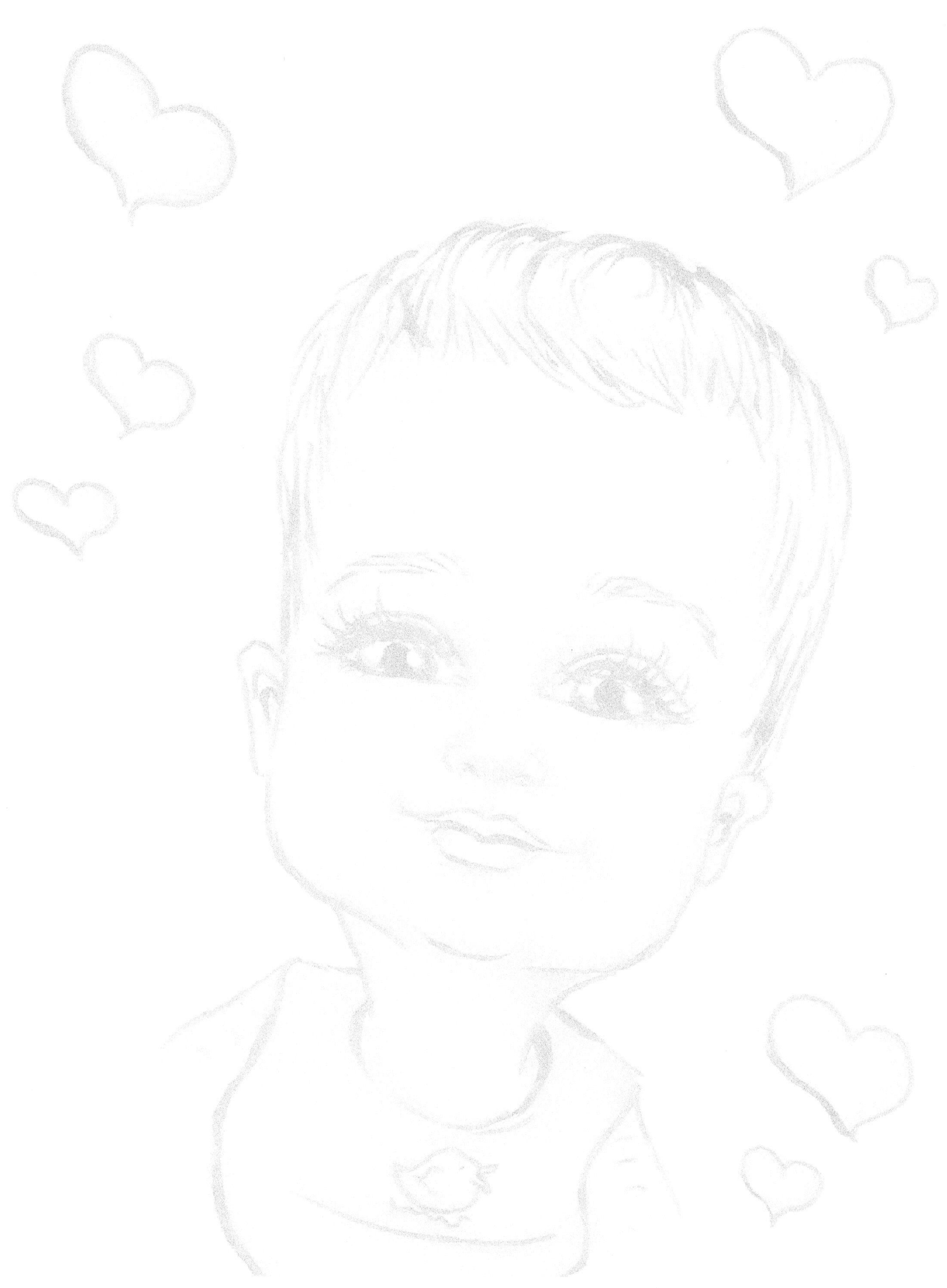

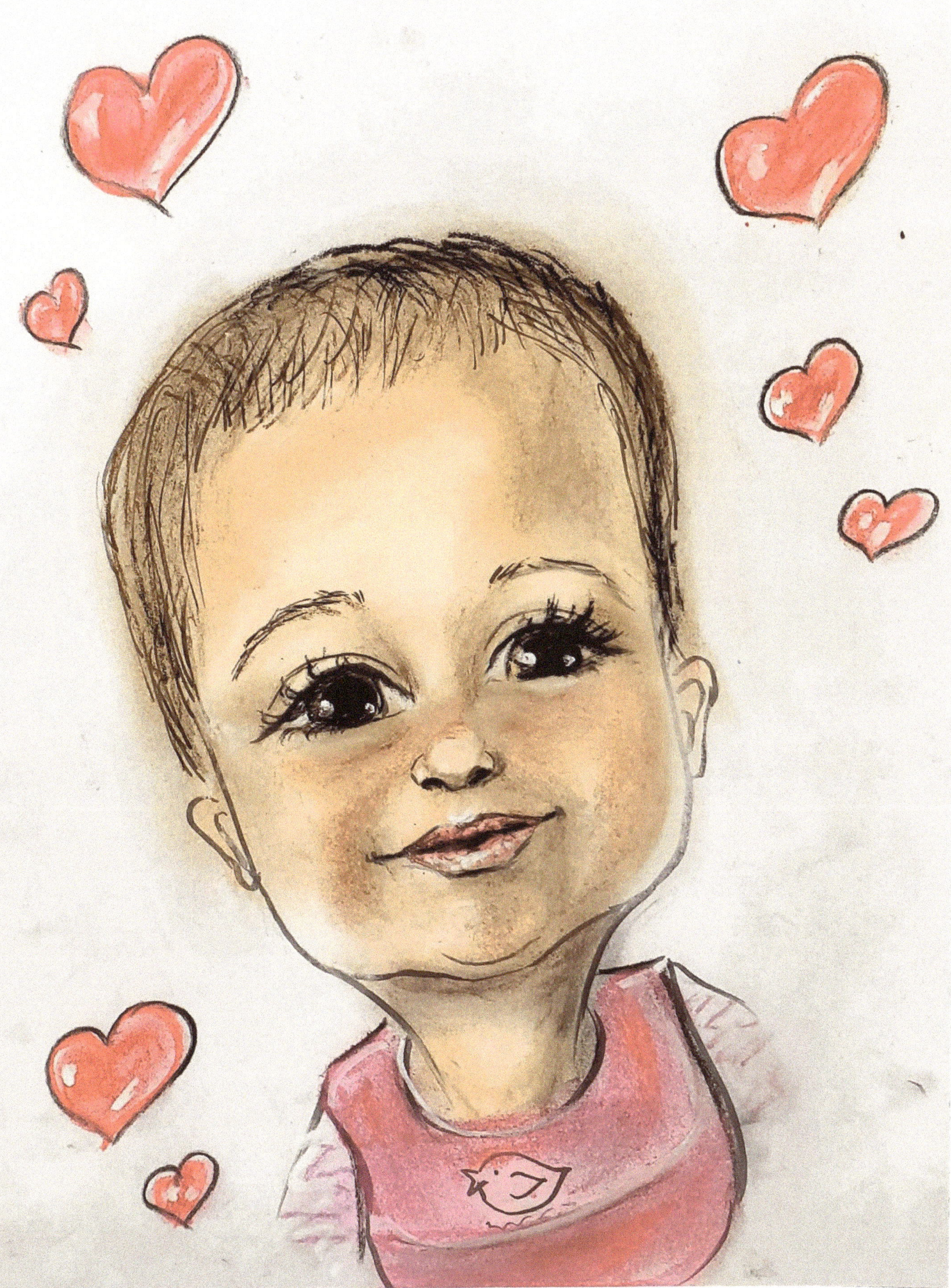

When drawing babies and children, imagine your own children or the children of those you are close to, and draw them with love and care.

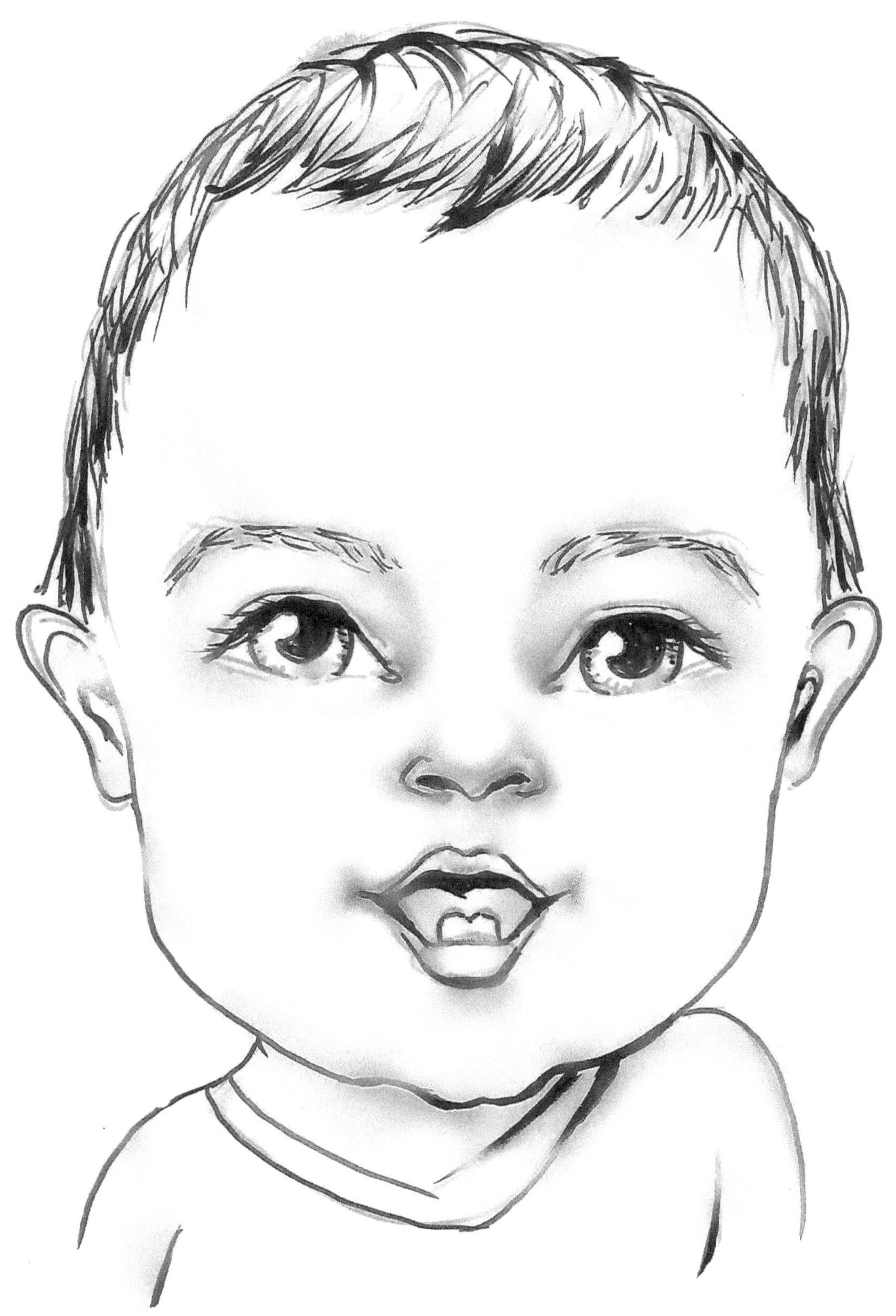

Trace

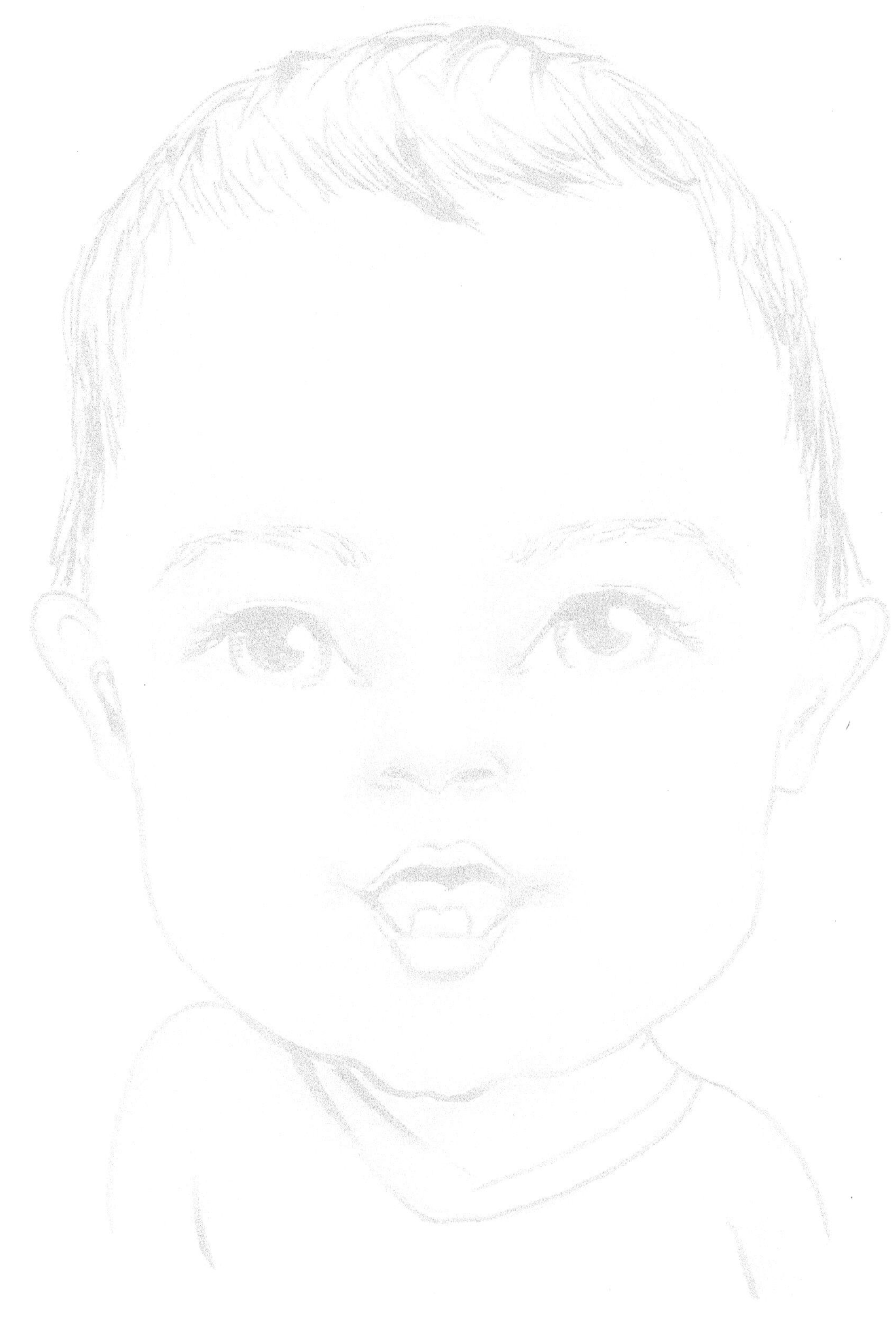

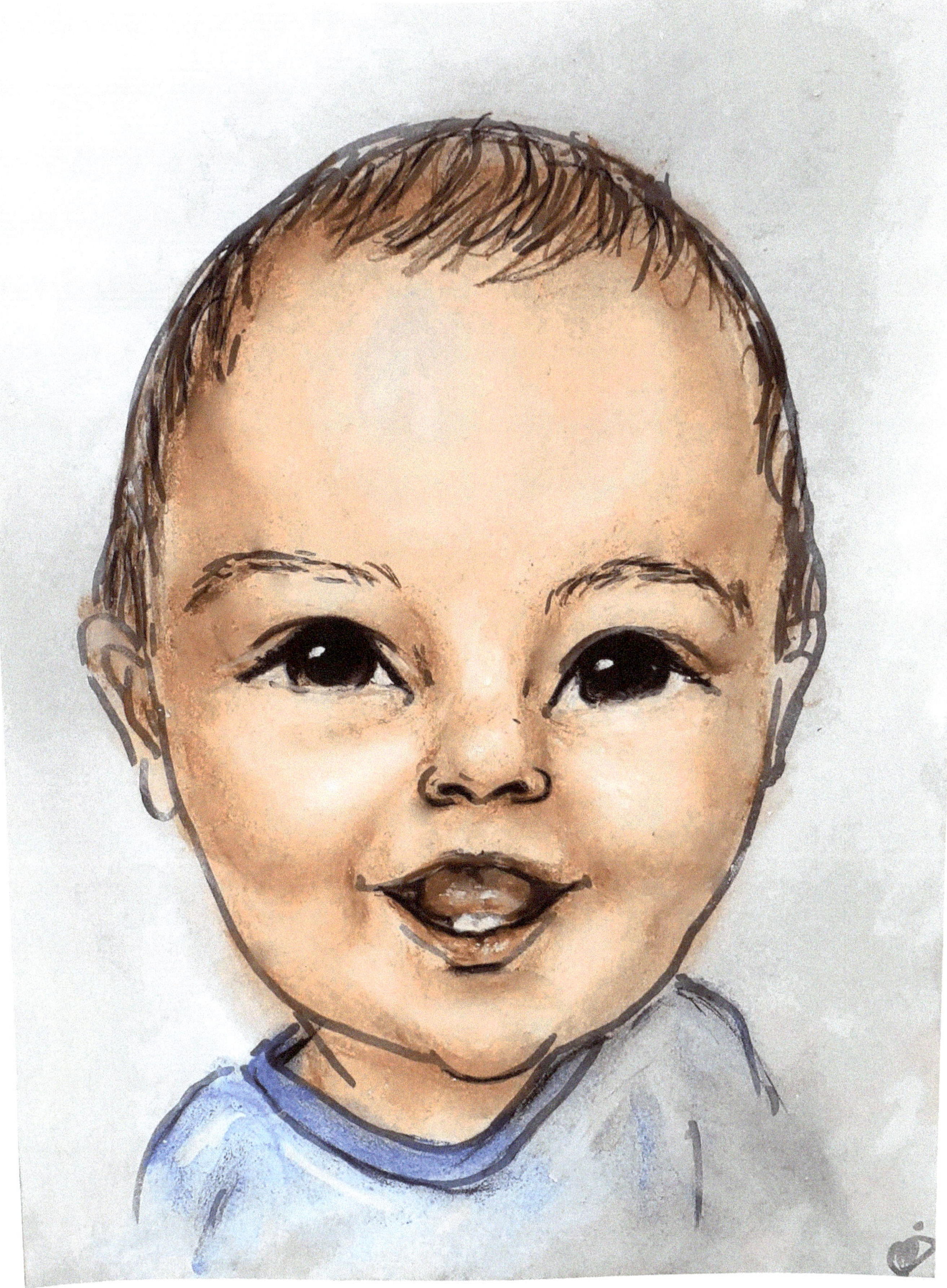

When coloring with soft
pastels, I enjoy painting in flat
areas of color and blending
them together later on.

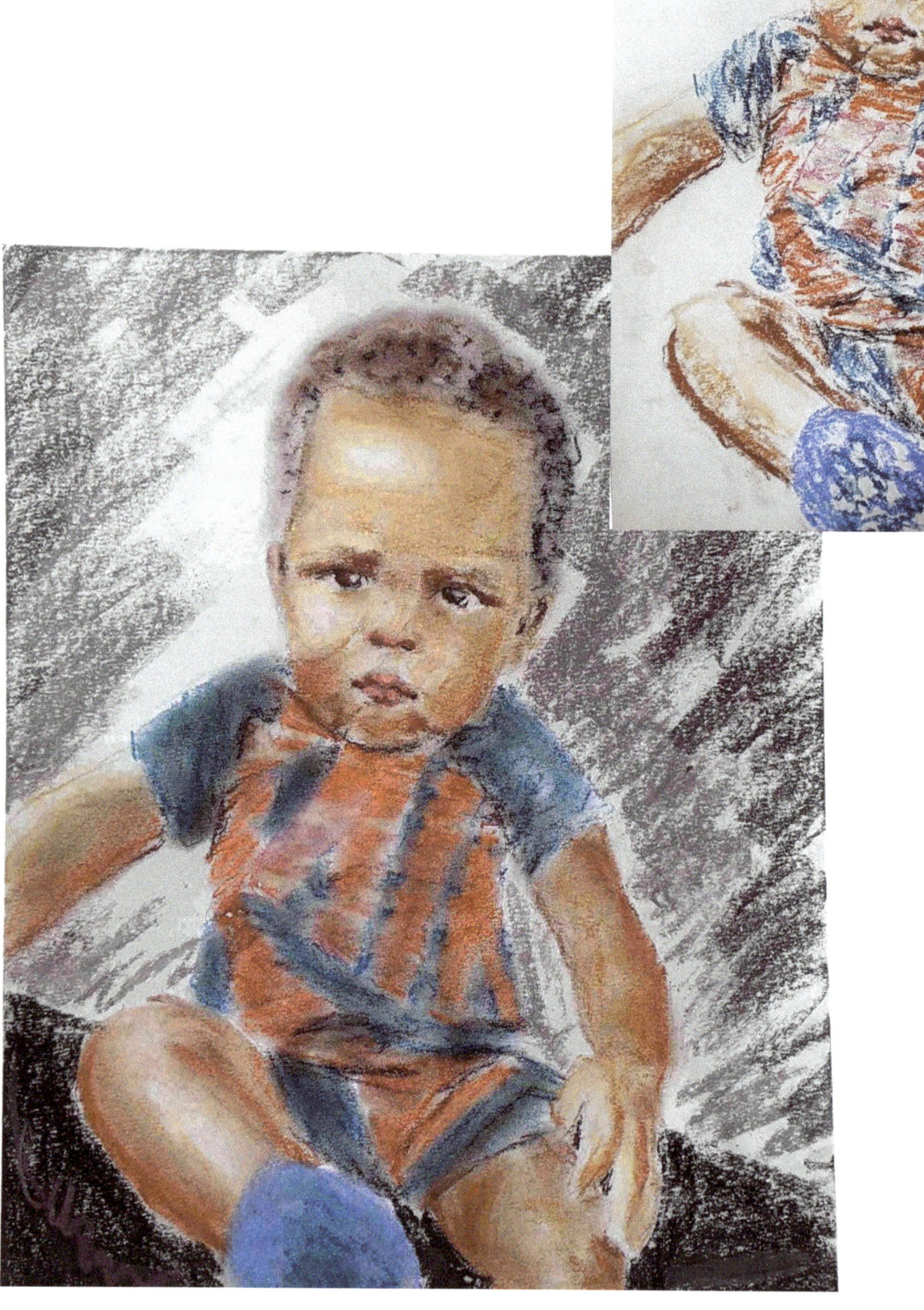

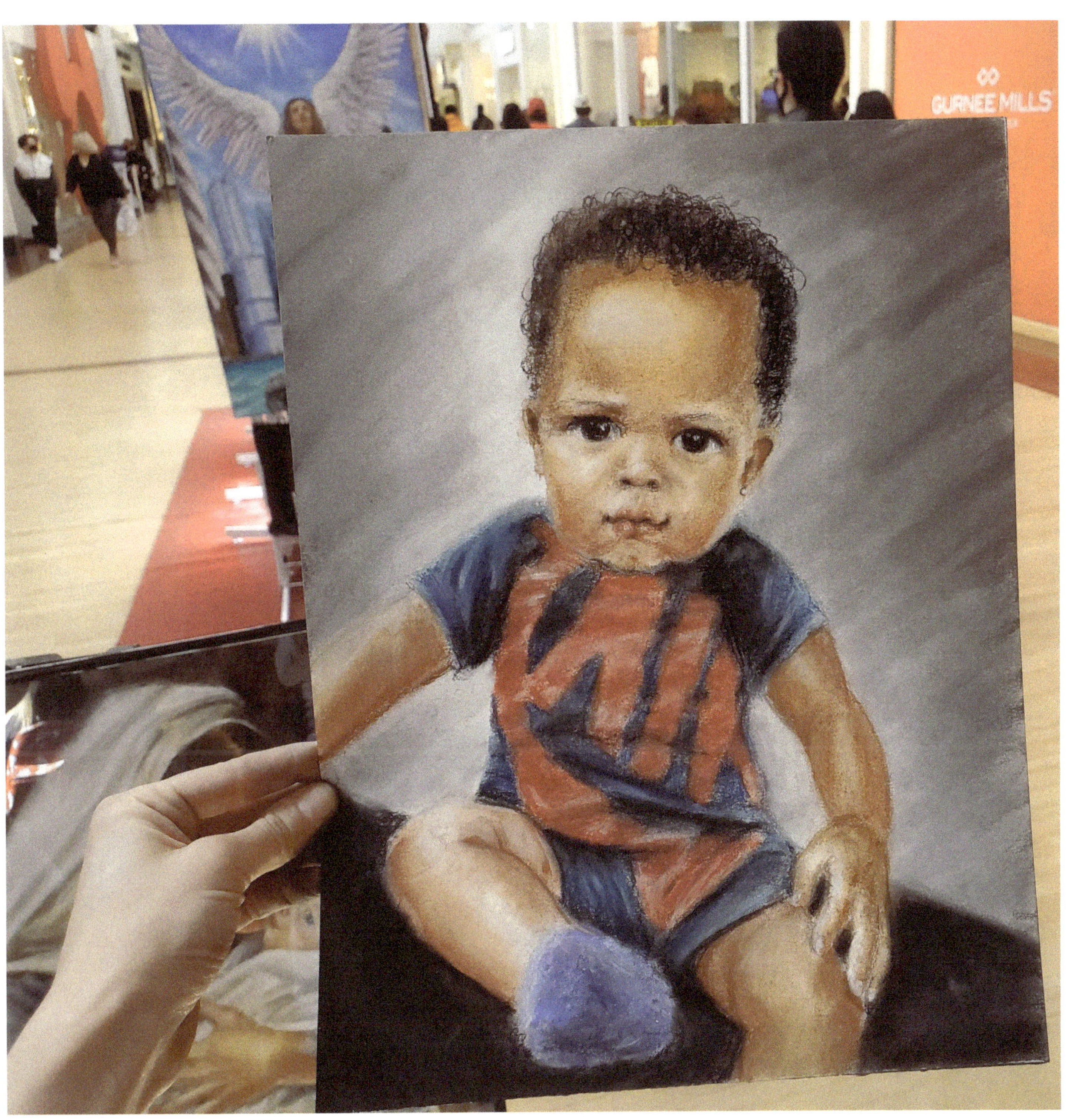

GURNEE MILLS

Coloring provides an outlet for emotional expression.
Coloring babies will very likely evoke positive thoughts
and emotions.

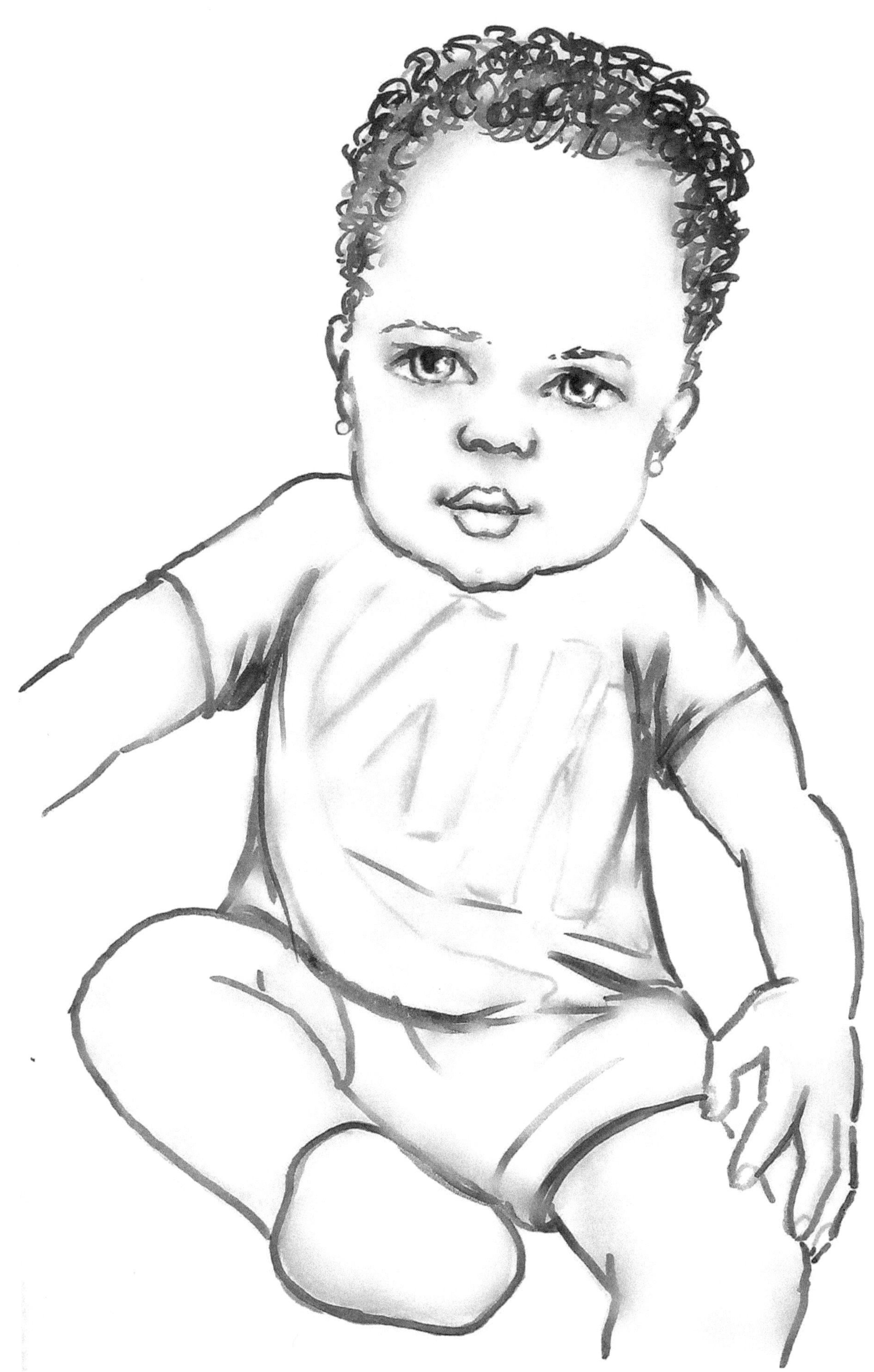
Color

Trace

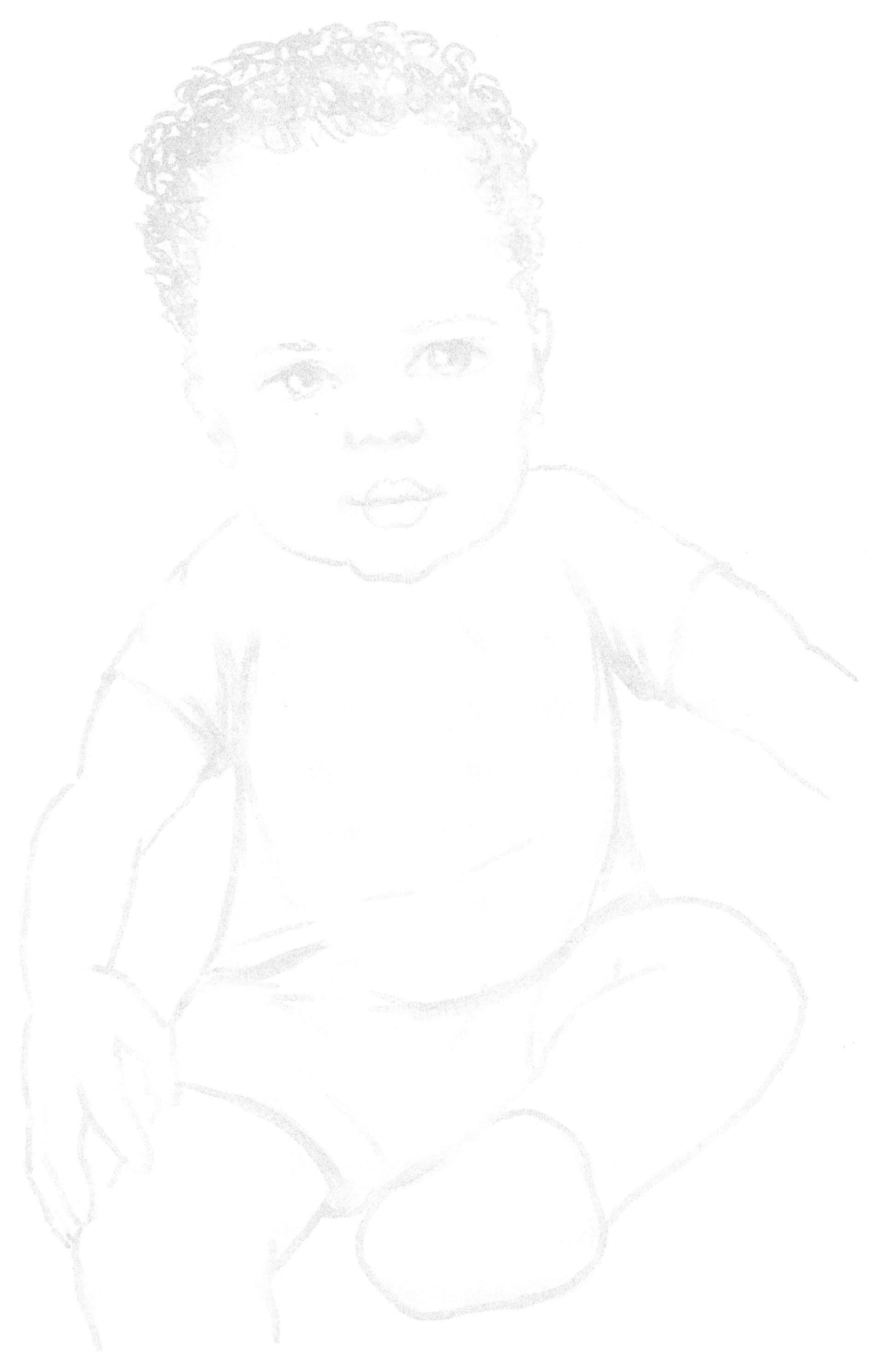

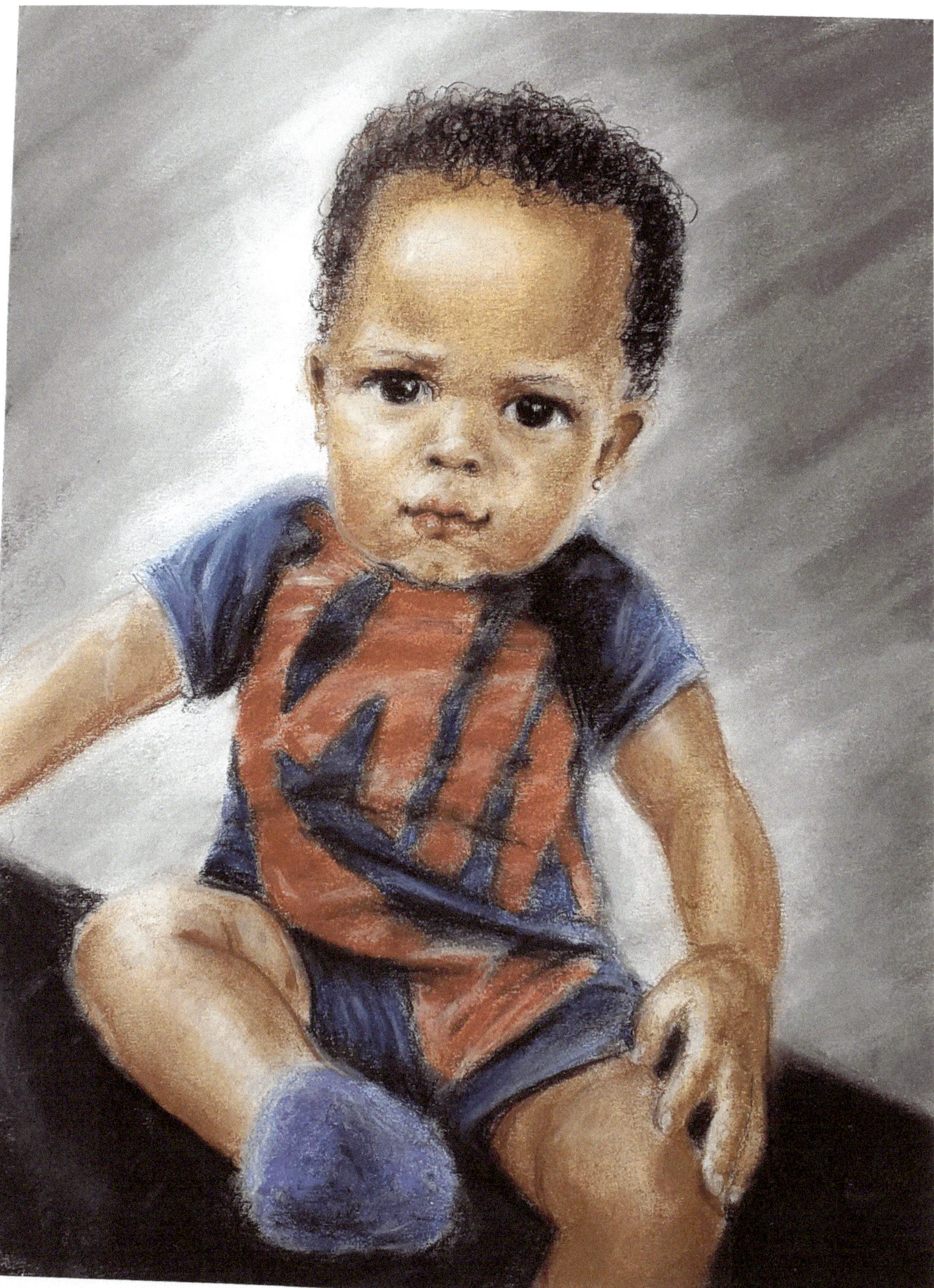

Sometimes simple cartoon drawings are best. You can draw them spontaneously and without pressure because they are not supposed to be realistic.

I draw cartoon-style art during live caricature entertainment events.

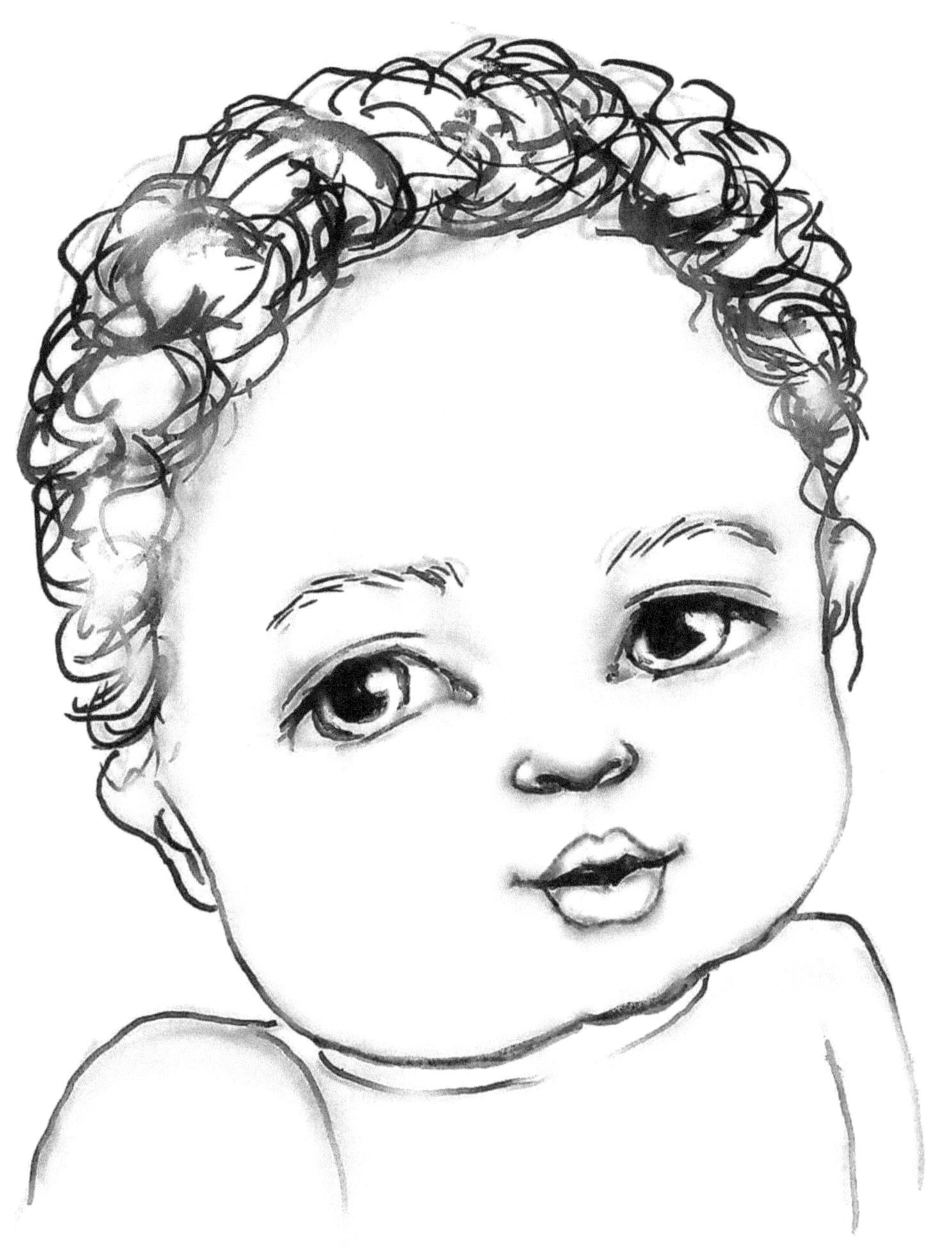

Trace

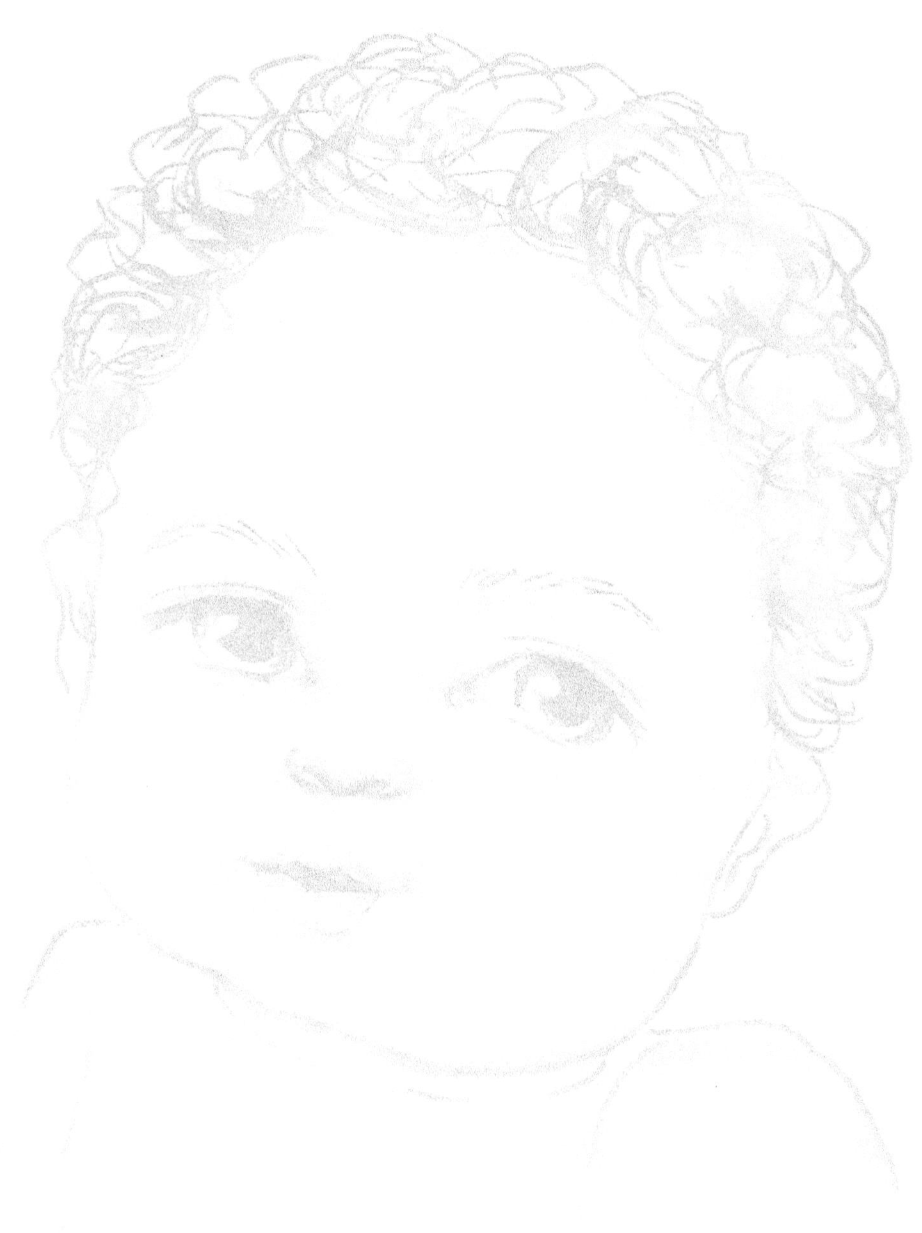

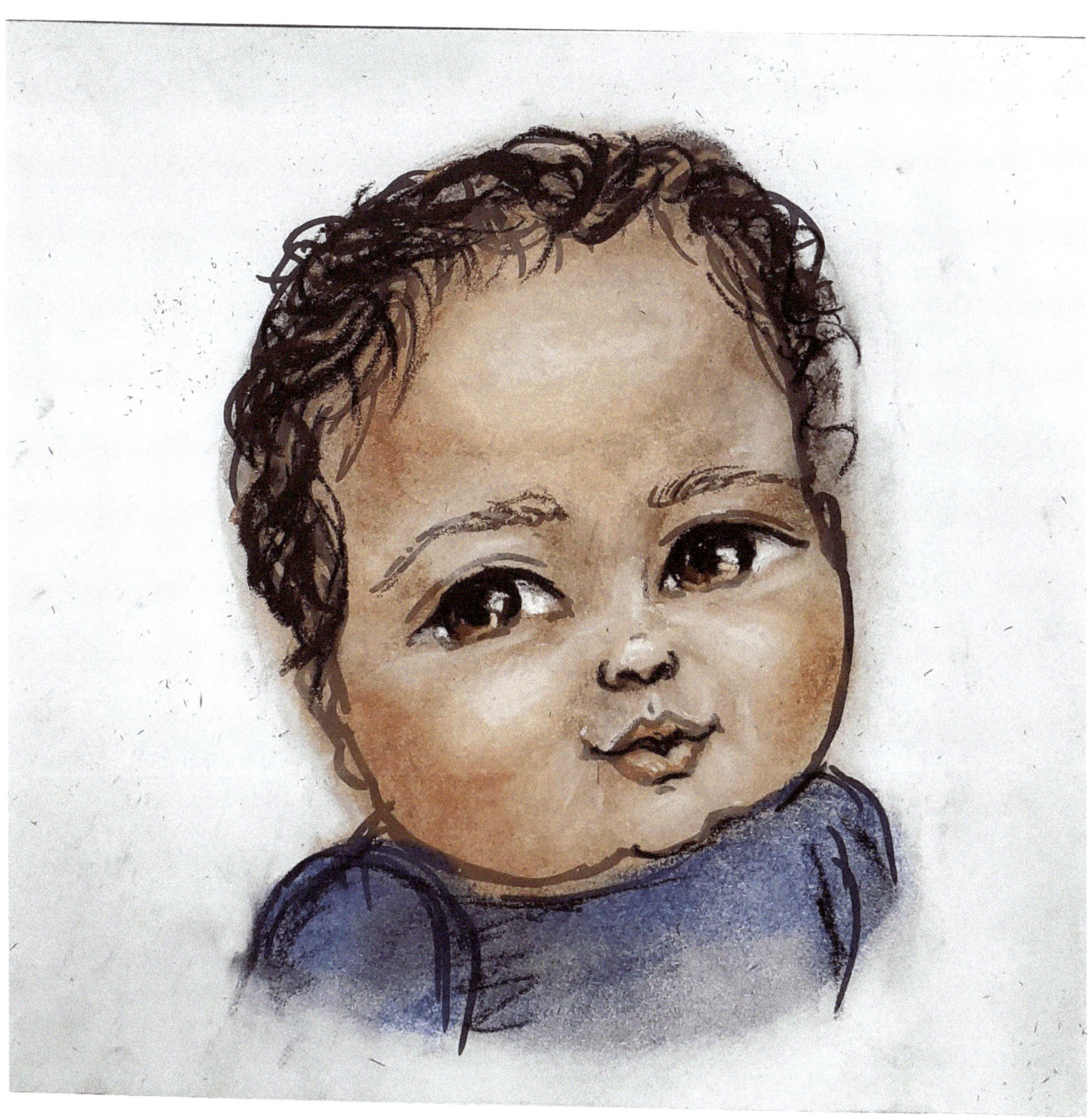

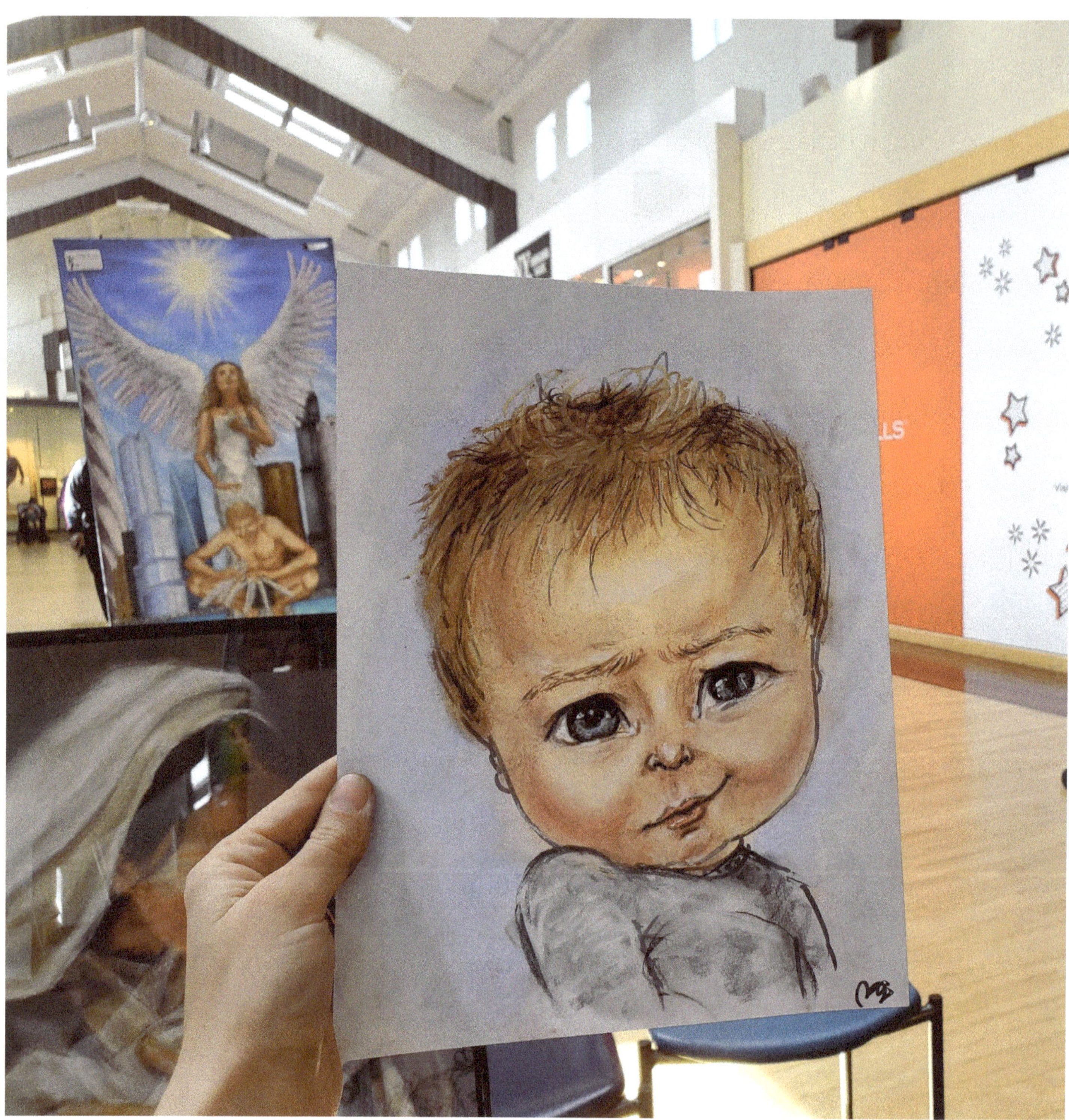

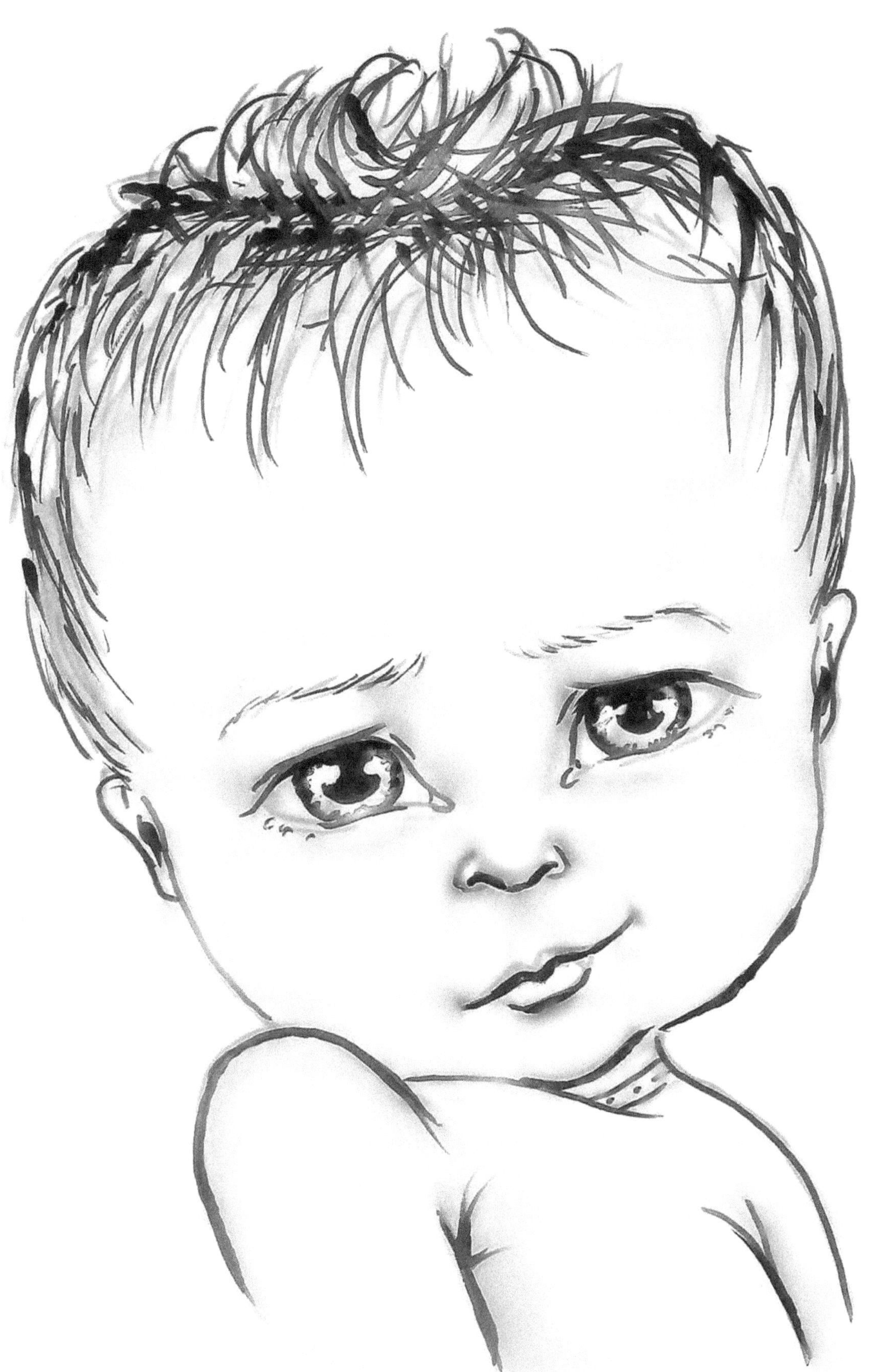

Trace

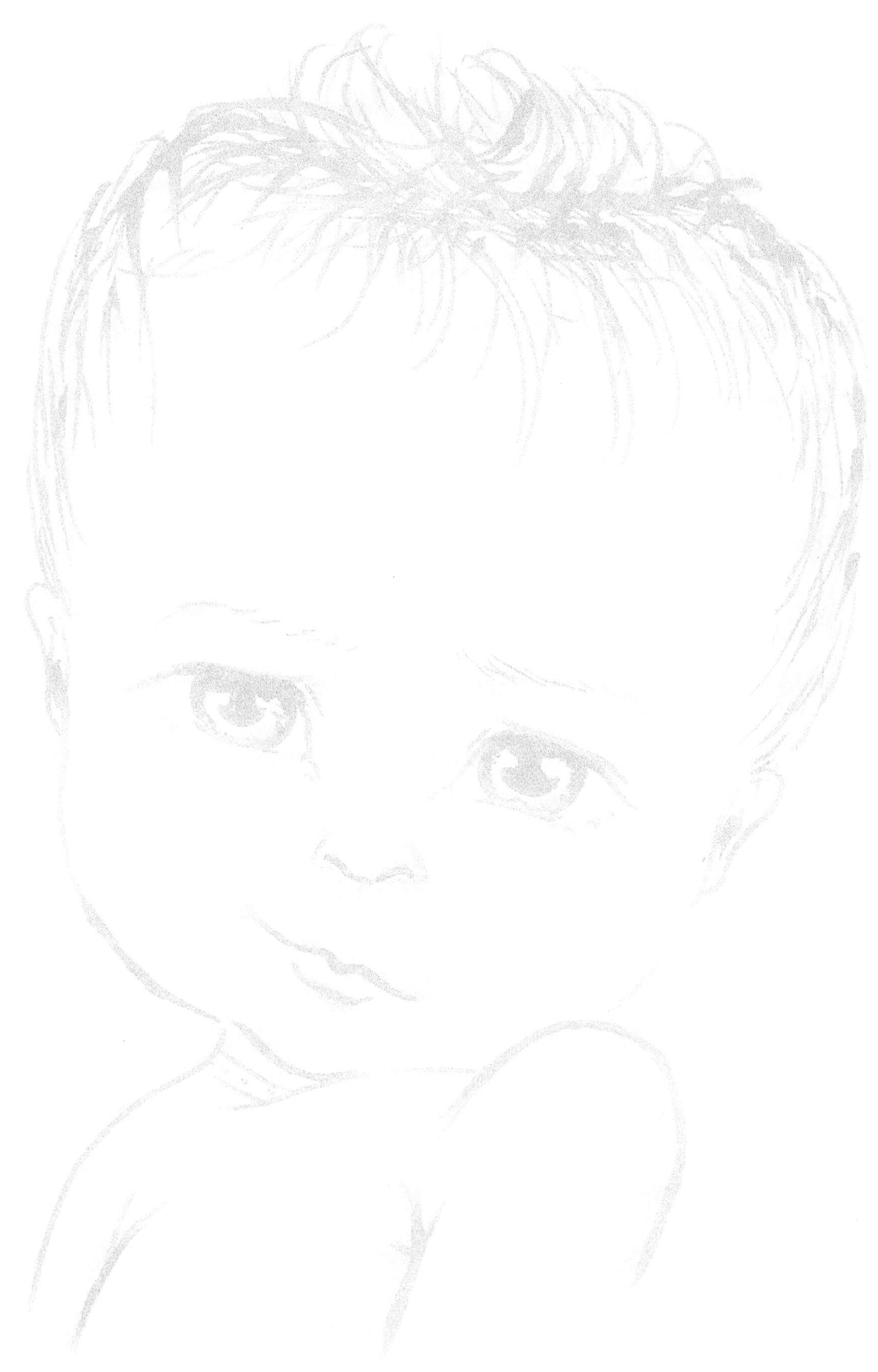

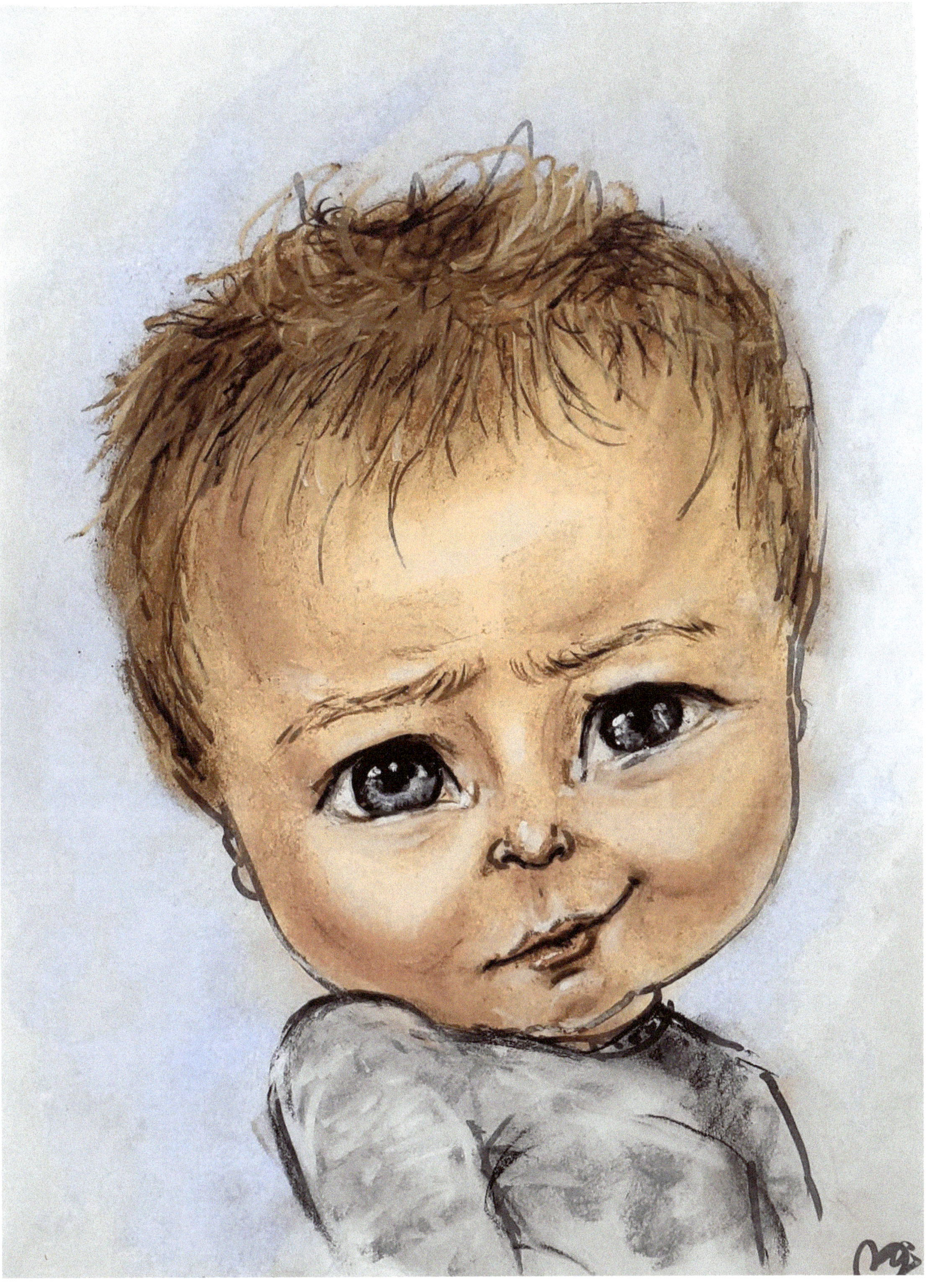

Imagine seeing yourself as a cool cartoon drawing
or as a funny and cute caricature when you were a
child. It would certainly bring joy to any child's face

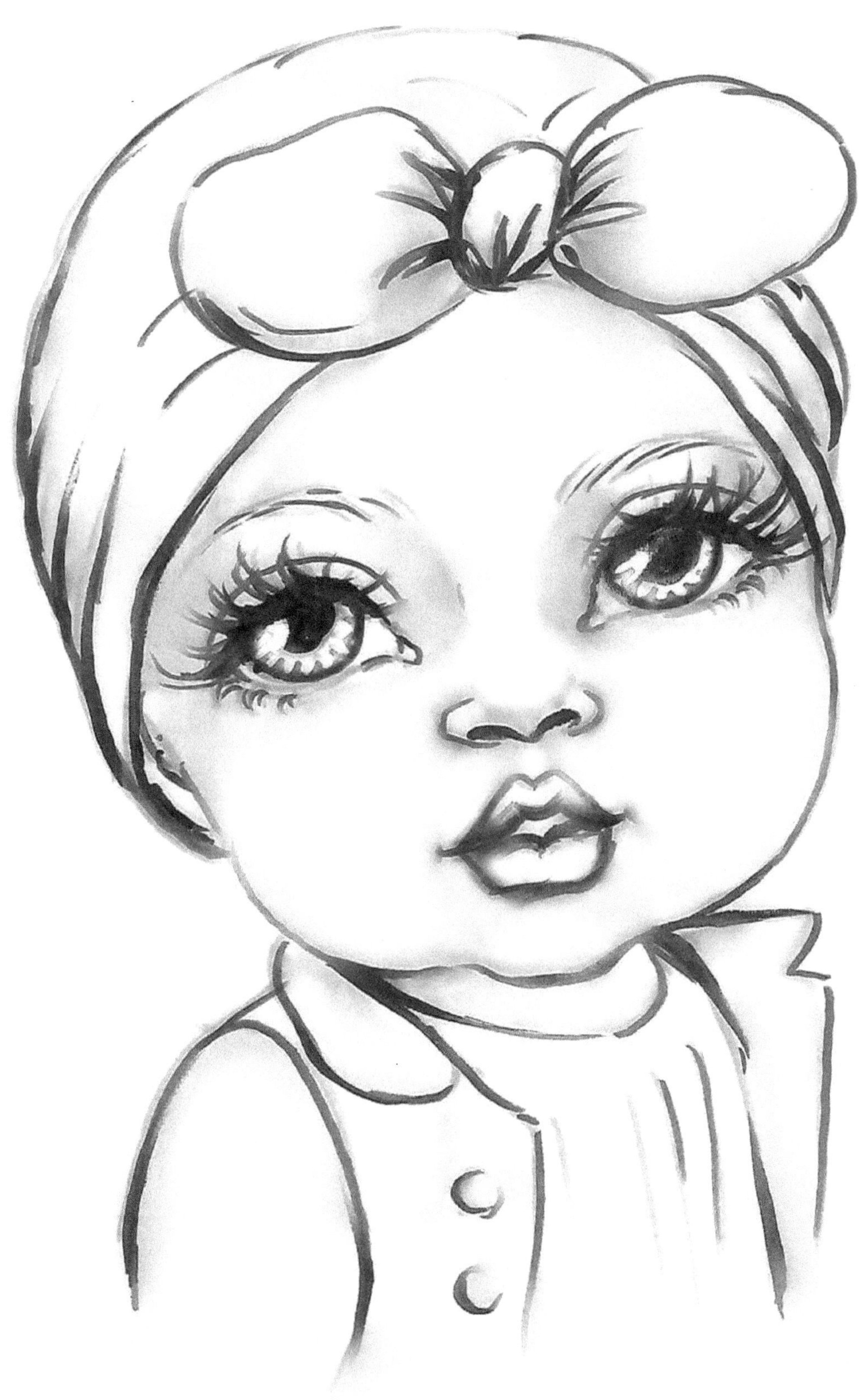

Trace

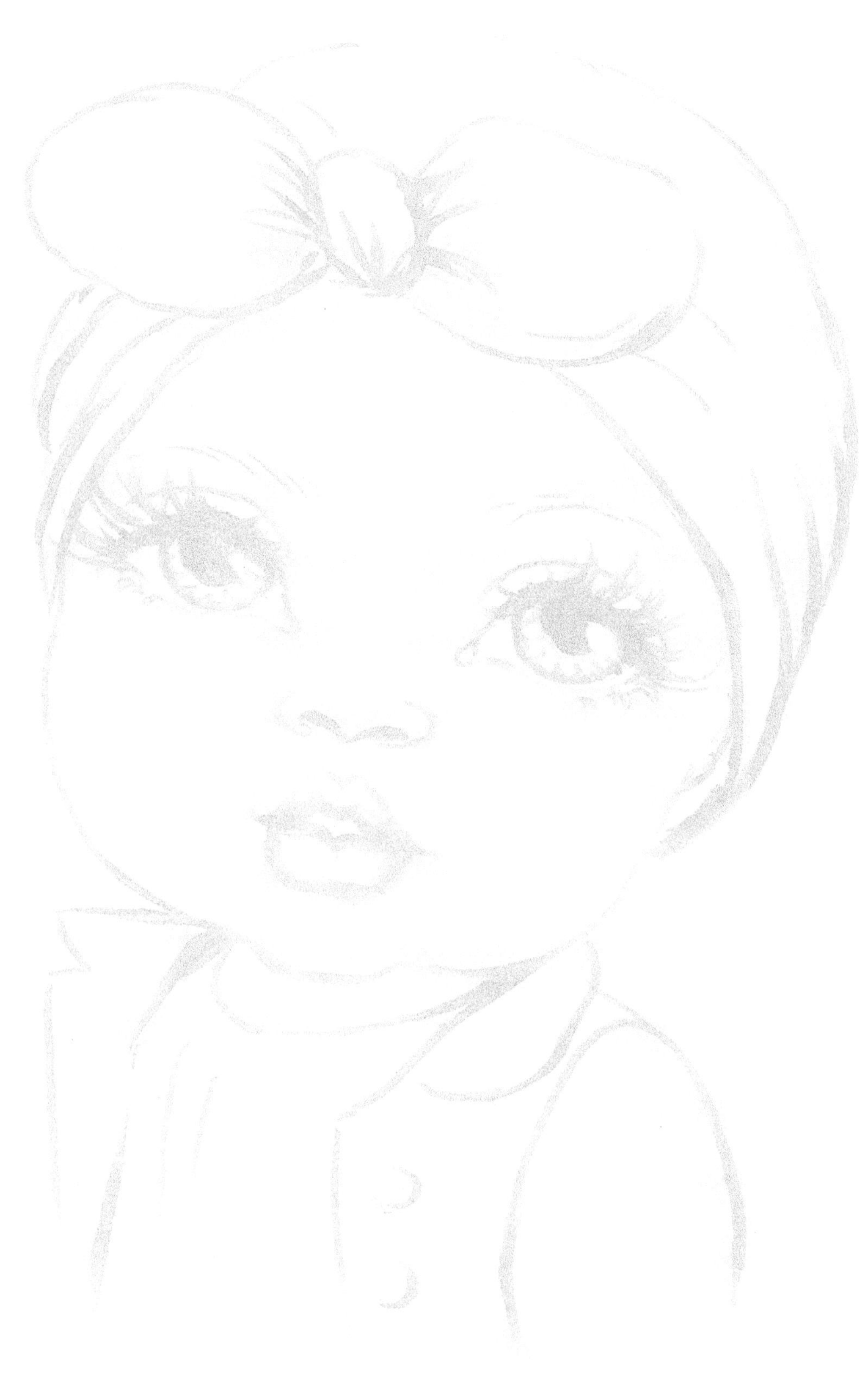

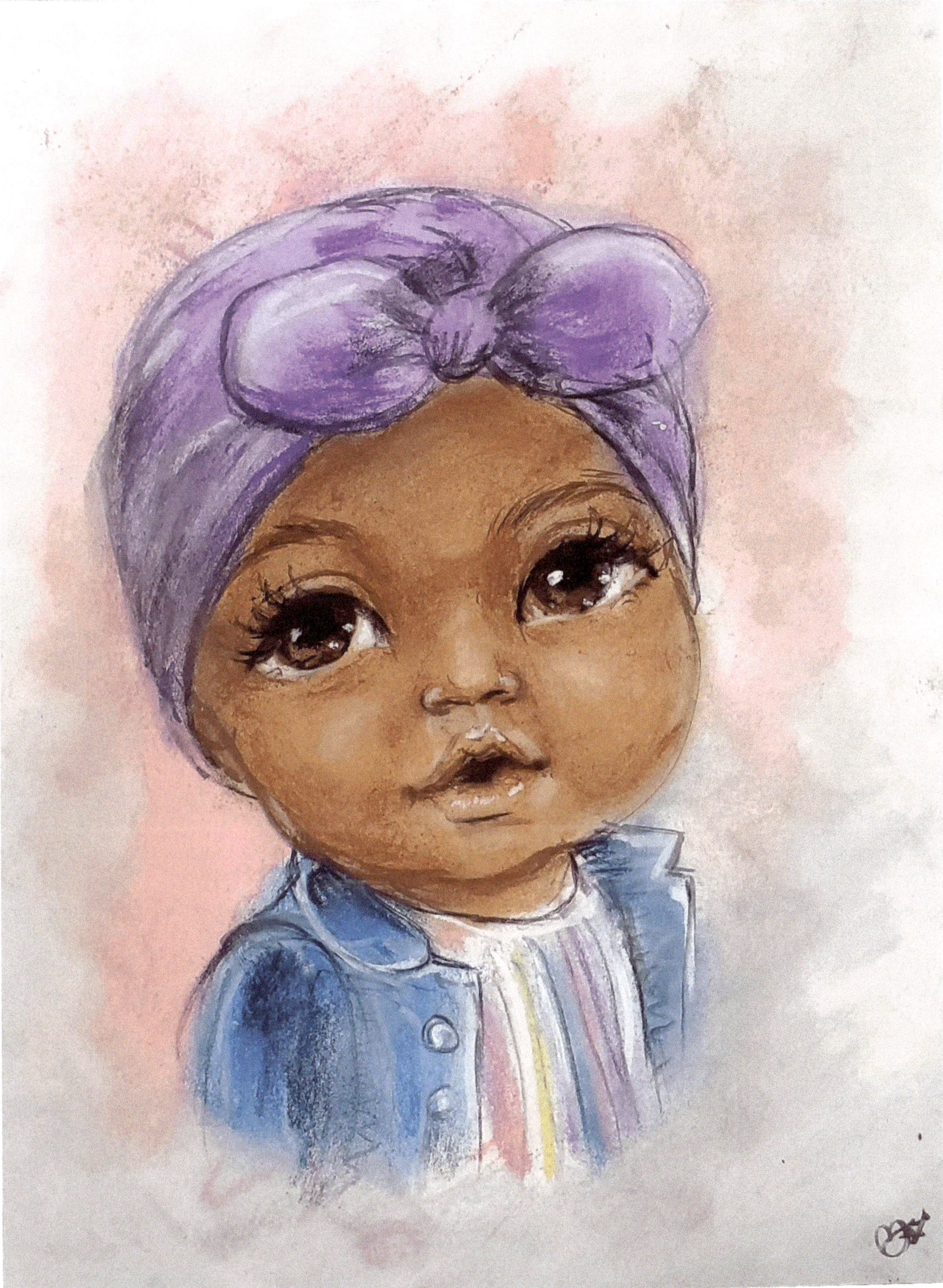

Consider drawing the babies in your family. Cartoon,
caricature art, and portraiture can be thoughtful and precious
gifts for a special occasion.

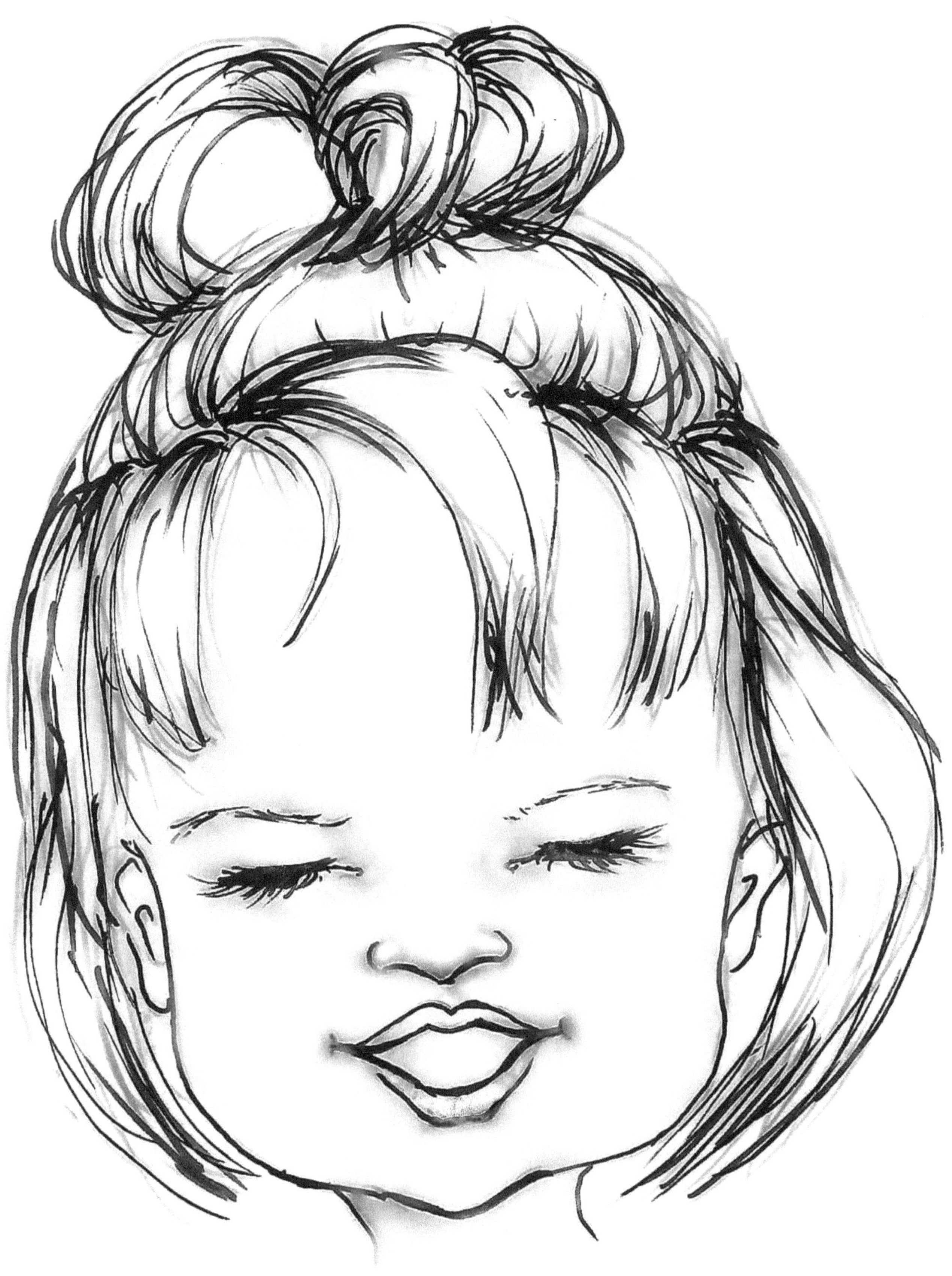

Color

Trace

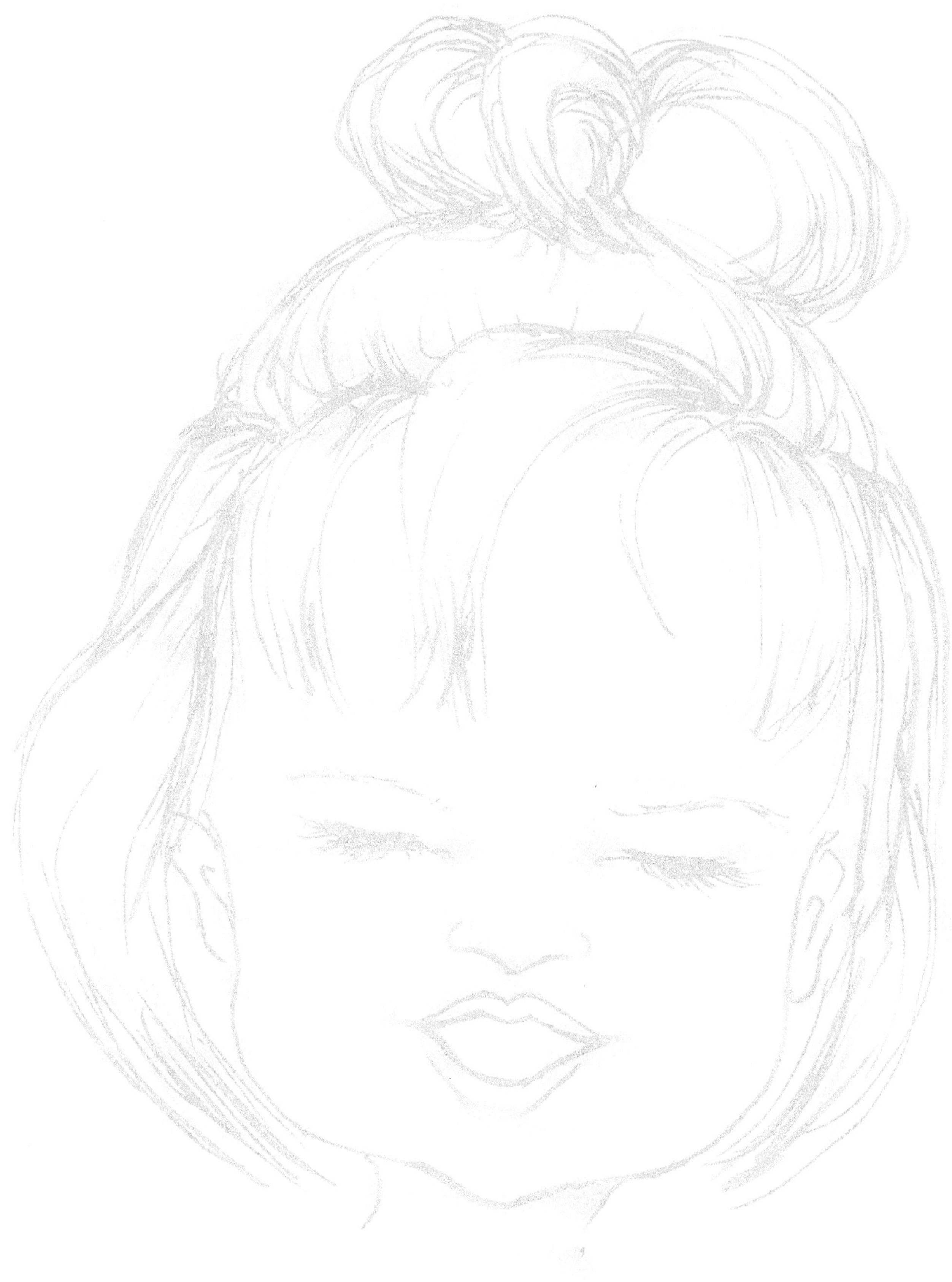

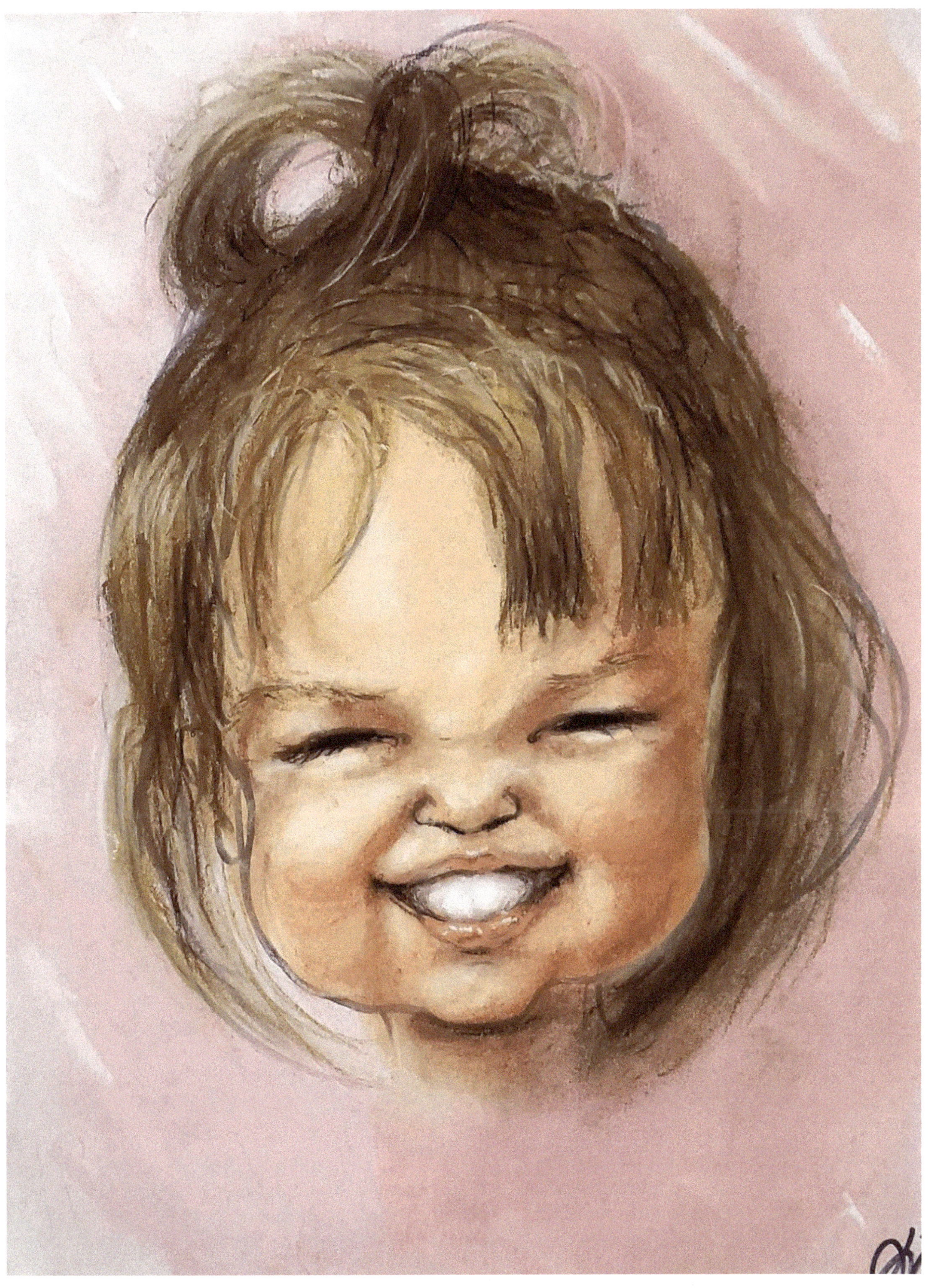

Have fun with simple, cute, and funny caricatures. Use this page to draw a similar artwork on your own. You can measure and compare the drawings using a pencil, the movement of your hand, or your eyesight. You can also draw a grid on both pages.

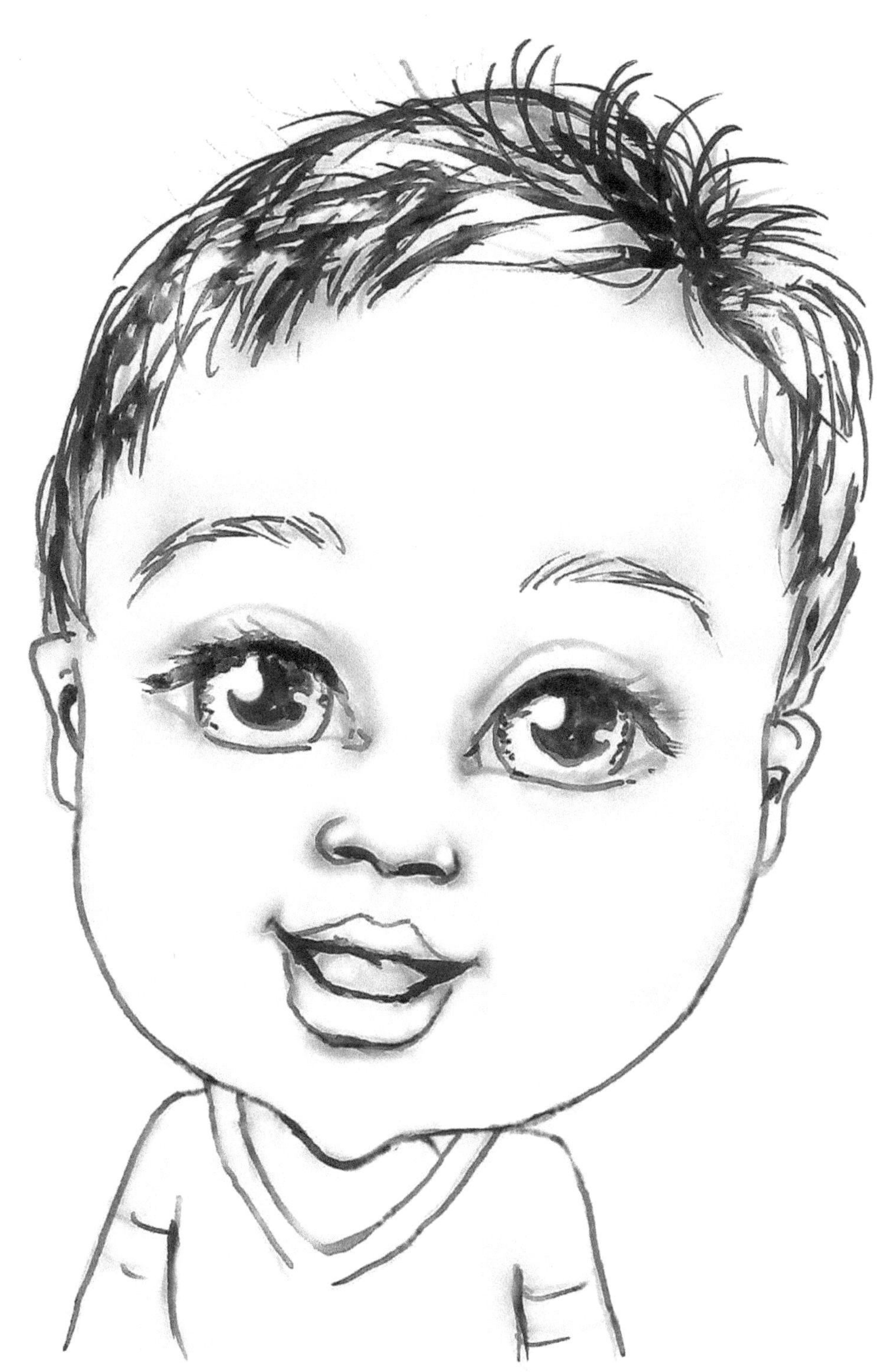

Trace

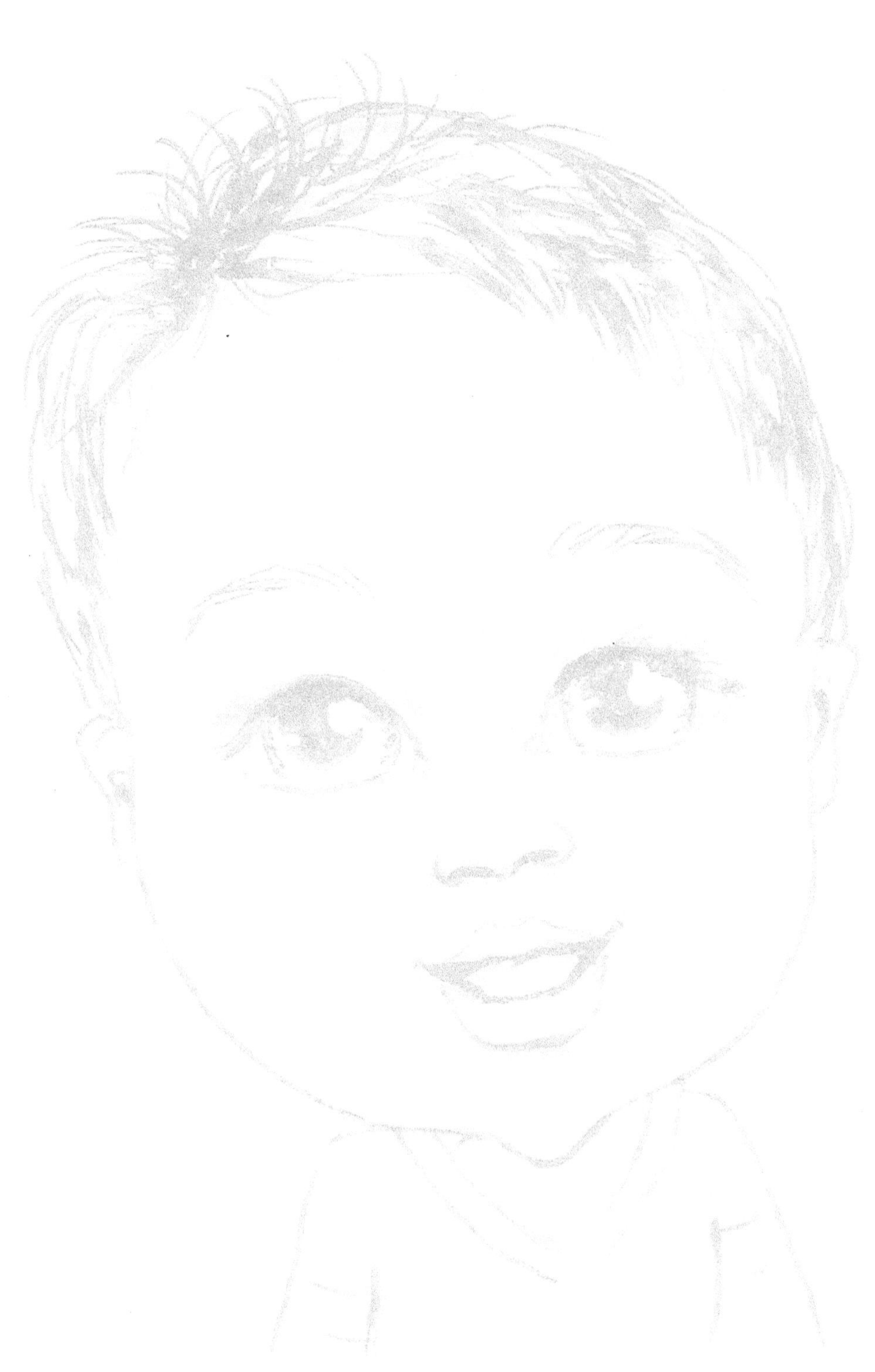

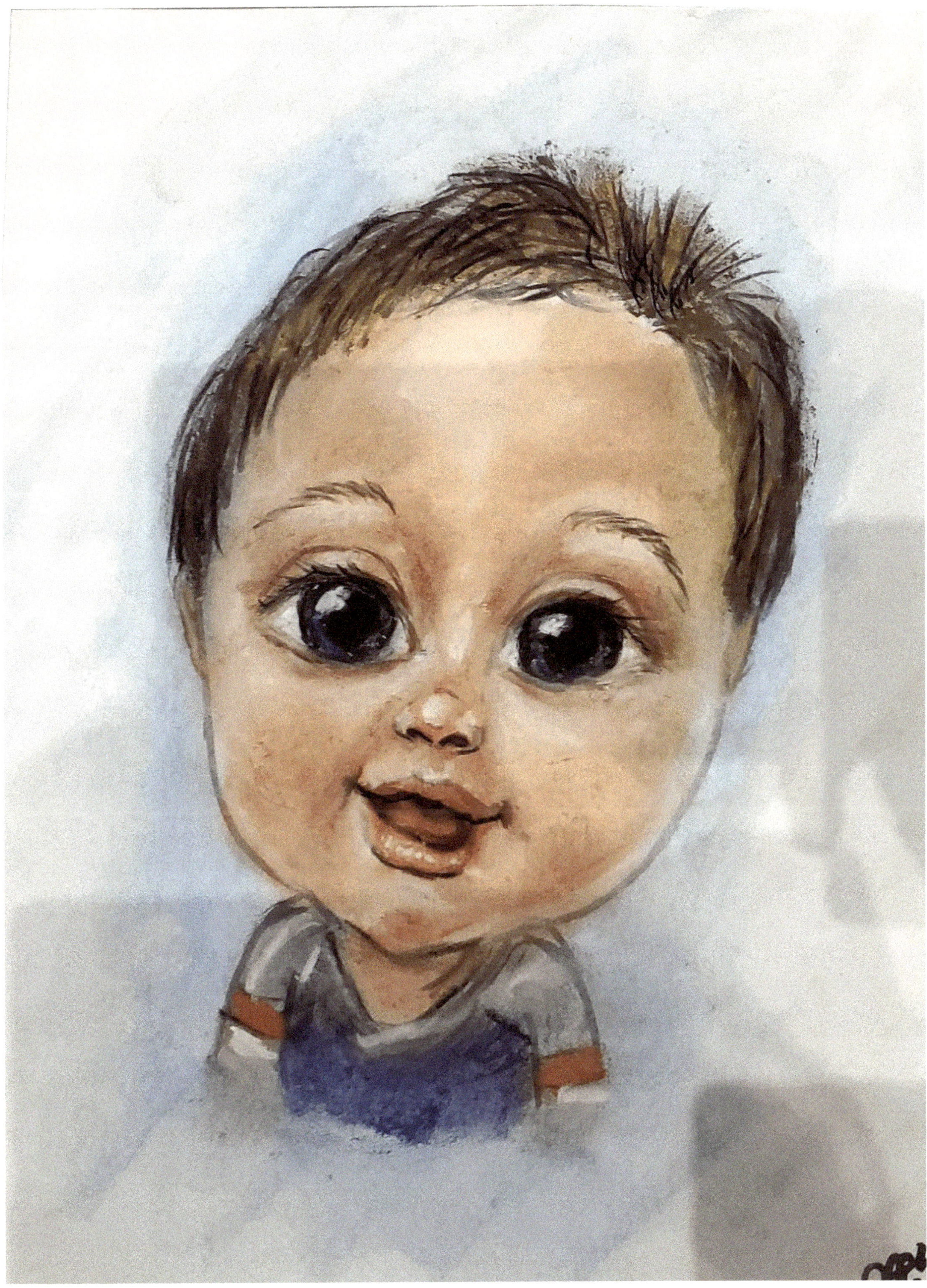

Coloring, tracing, and drawing adorable babies may
increase your sense of happiness and pleasure

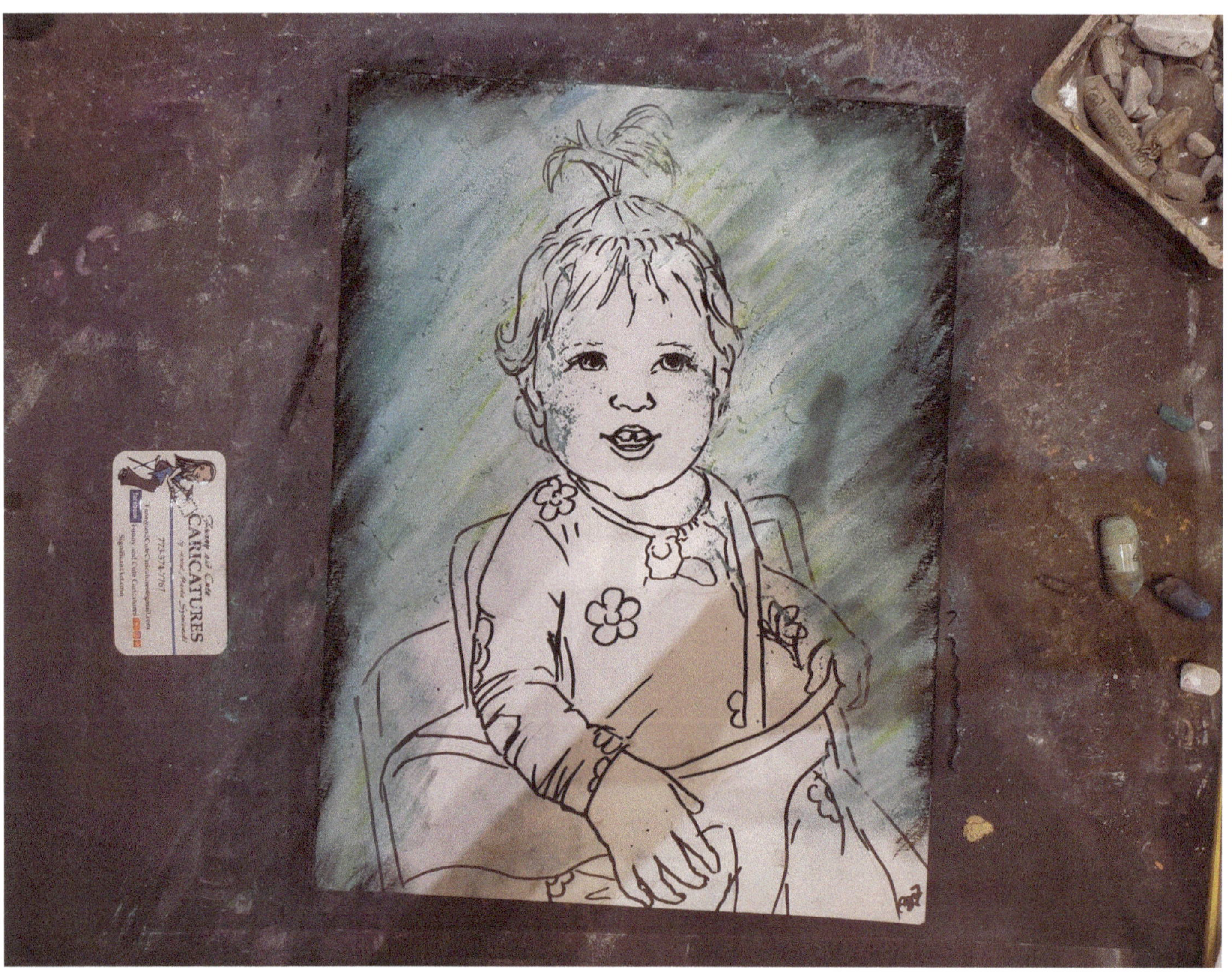

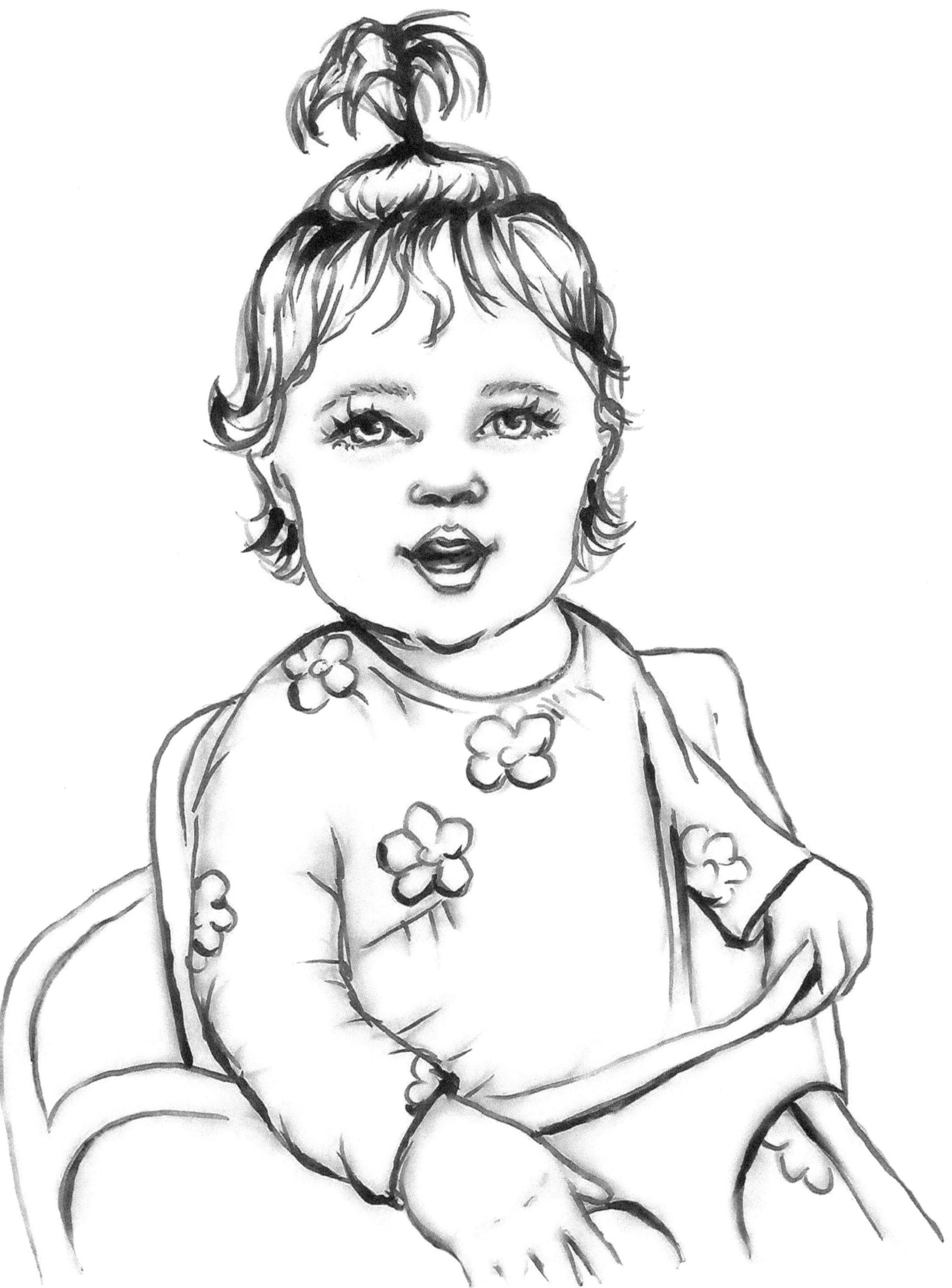

Trace

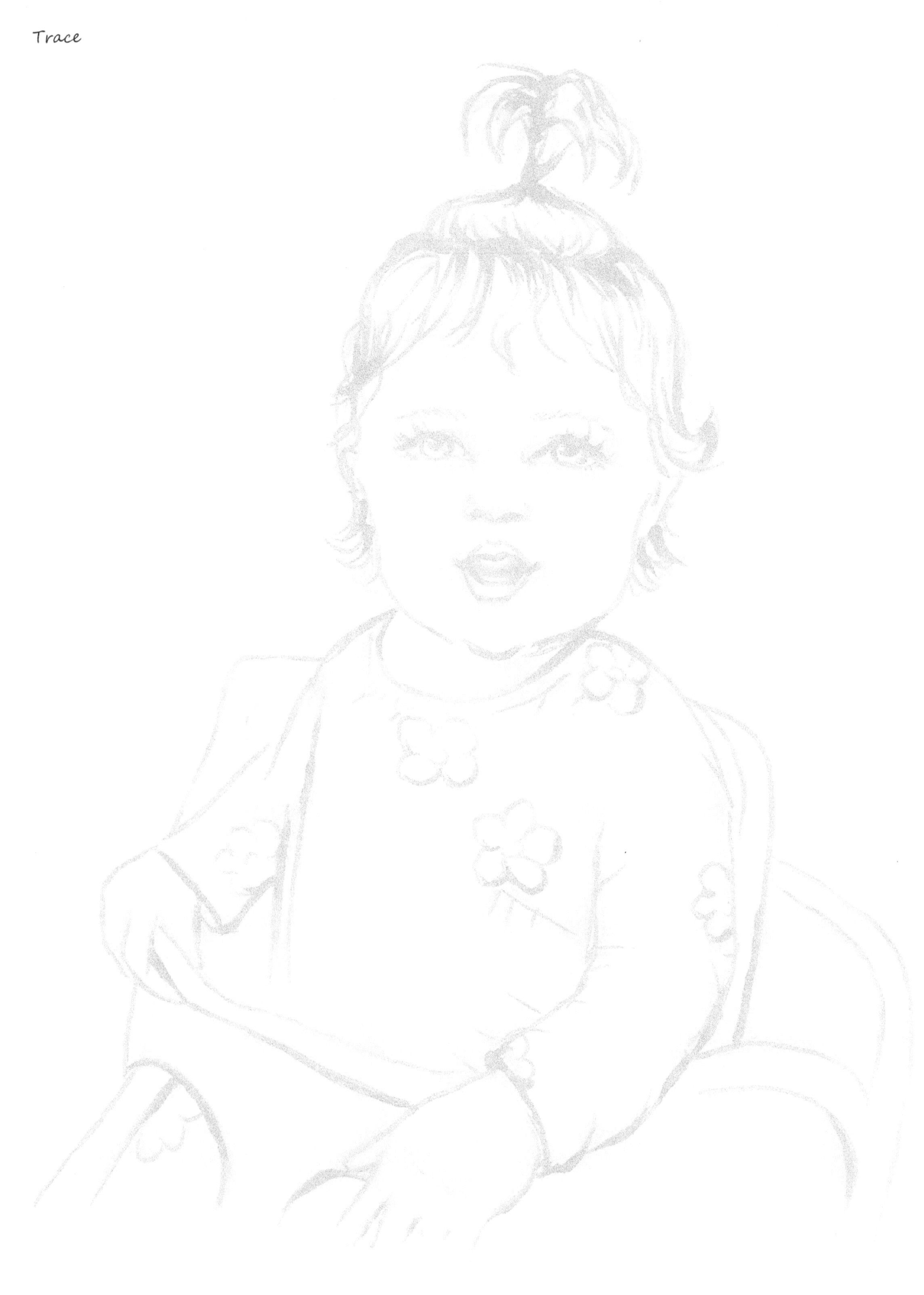

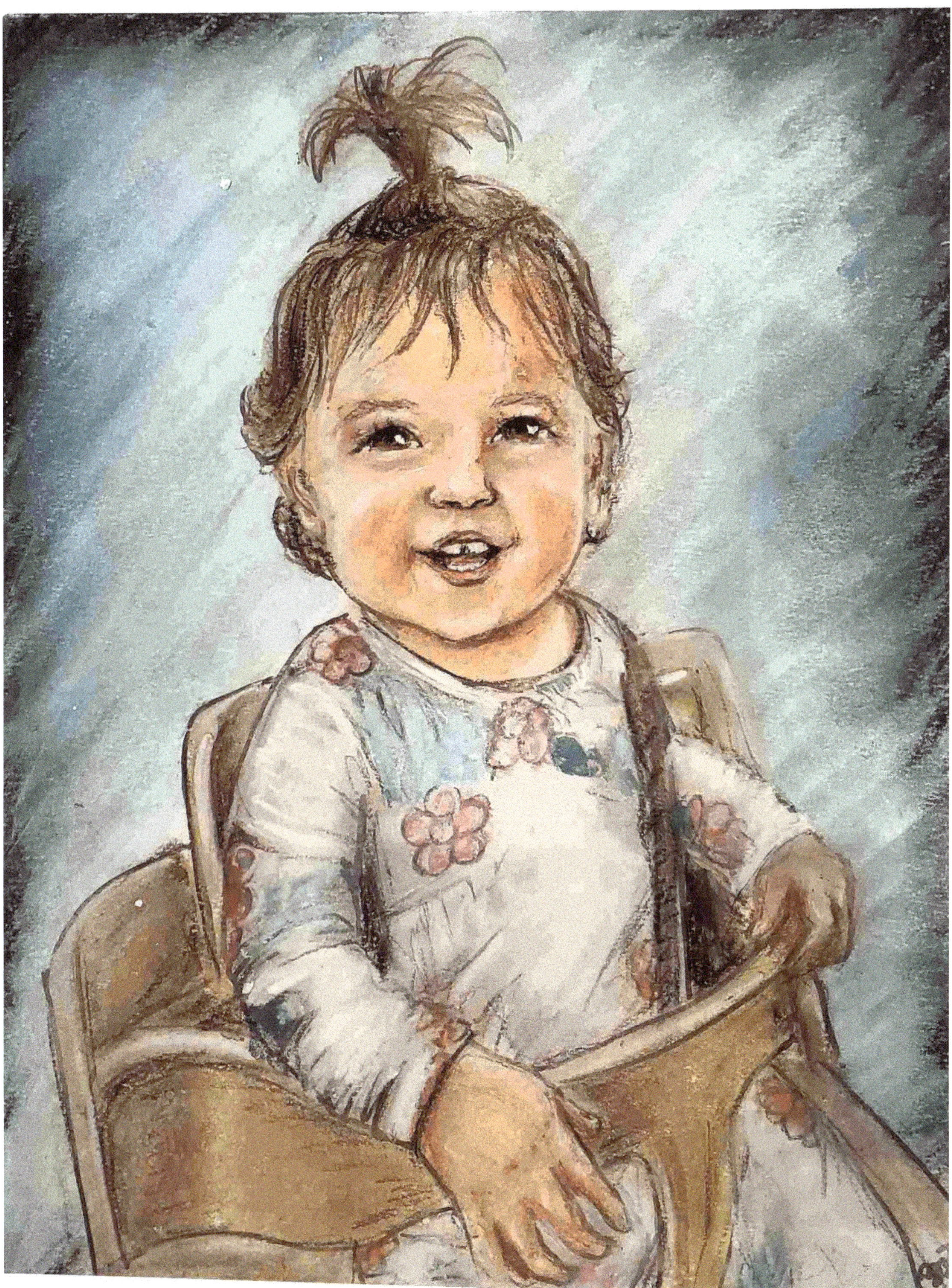

Thank You for Coloring,   Tracing, and Drawing with me

Please consider rating ★★★★★ and reviewing this book!

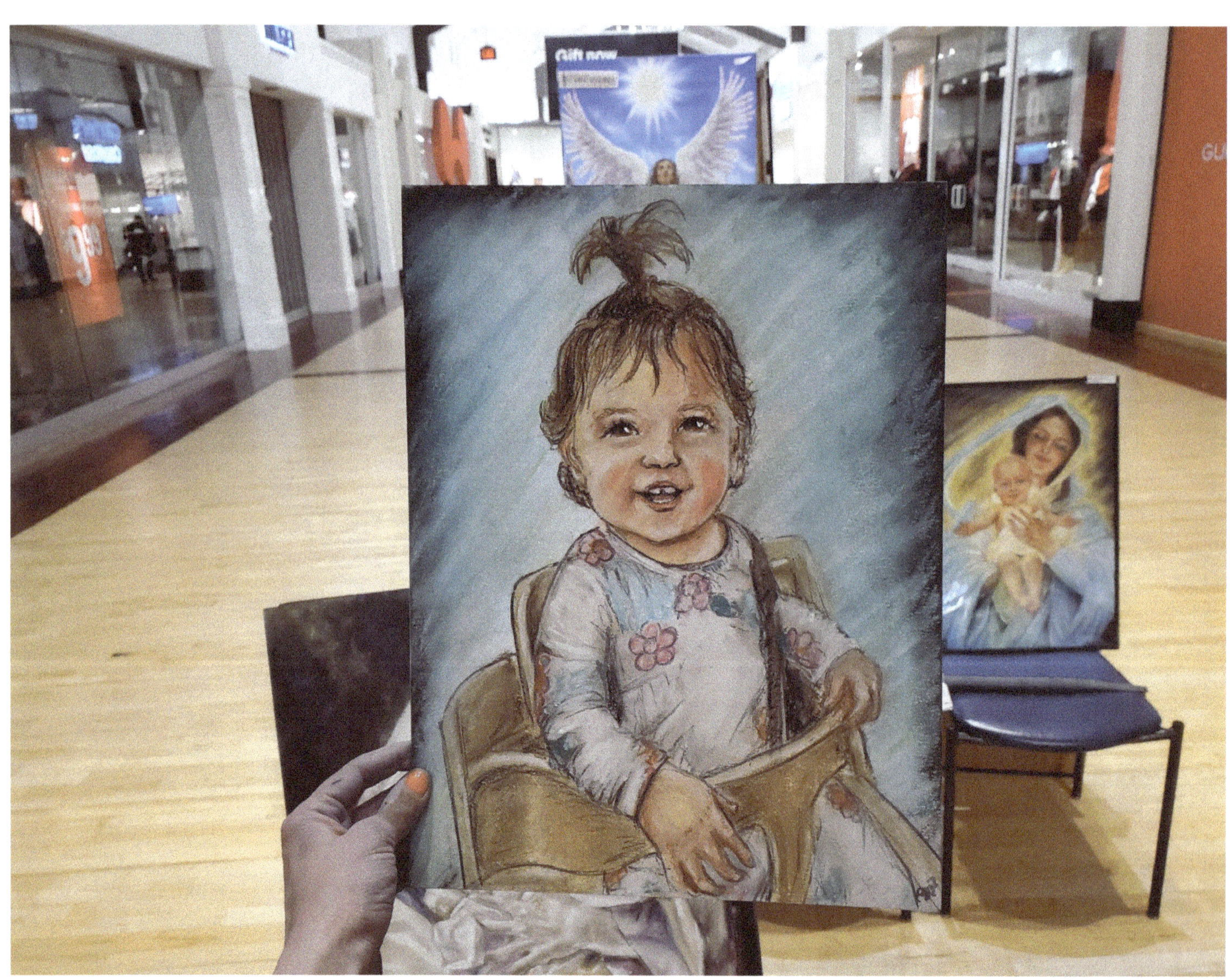

About the Artist

Marta Sytniewski is a professional artist. She has been trained in art:

☑ **academically** at Northeastern Illinois University,

☑ **independently** through literature and practice, which is how she came to study Classical European Portraiture and Figure Painting, and

☑ **privately** through an apprenticeship with her mother, Anna Jelen, MFA, since early childhood.

In her early career, Marta specialized in traditional oil painting, with elaborate, large-scale narrative compositions; sacred art, and murals. She frequently donated her work to charity and drew live event caricatures to encourage community engagement and fundraise for charity organizations.

Marta established her company, Funny And Cute Caricatures, in 2019 and has been drawing portraits and caricatures professionally in her fine art gallery at the Gurnee Mills Mall near Chicago, IL. Marta's traditional, handmade artwork is accomplished in fine art pastels, charcoal, graphite, acrylic, and oil paint.

When drawing portraits and caricatures, Marta looks for the best in the people that she is drawing, just like a mother sees her children—and in fact, she is a mother of three.

To order additional copies of this book, please contact:

Artist Marta Sytniewski

FunnyAndCuteCaricatures.com

FunnyAndCuteArt@gmail.com

www.facebook.com/FunnyAndCuteCaricatures

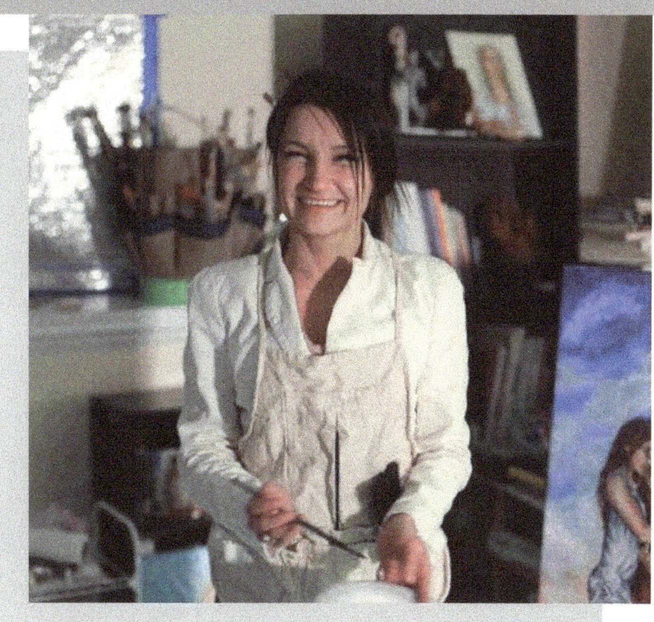

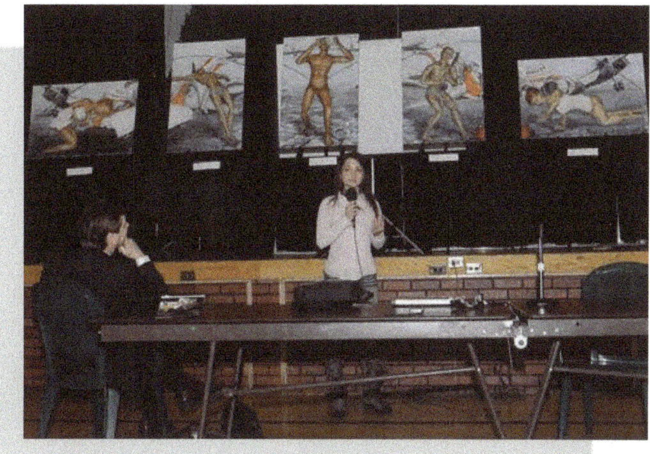

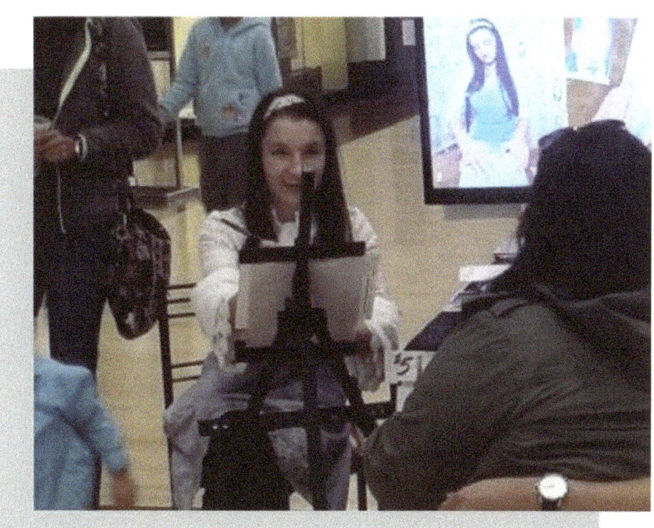

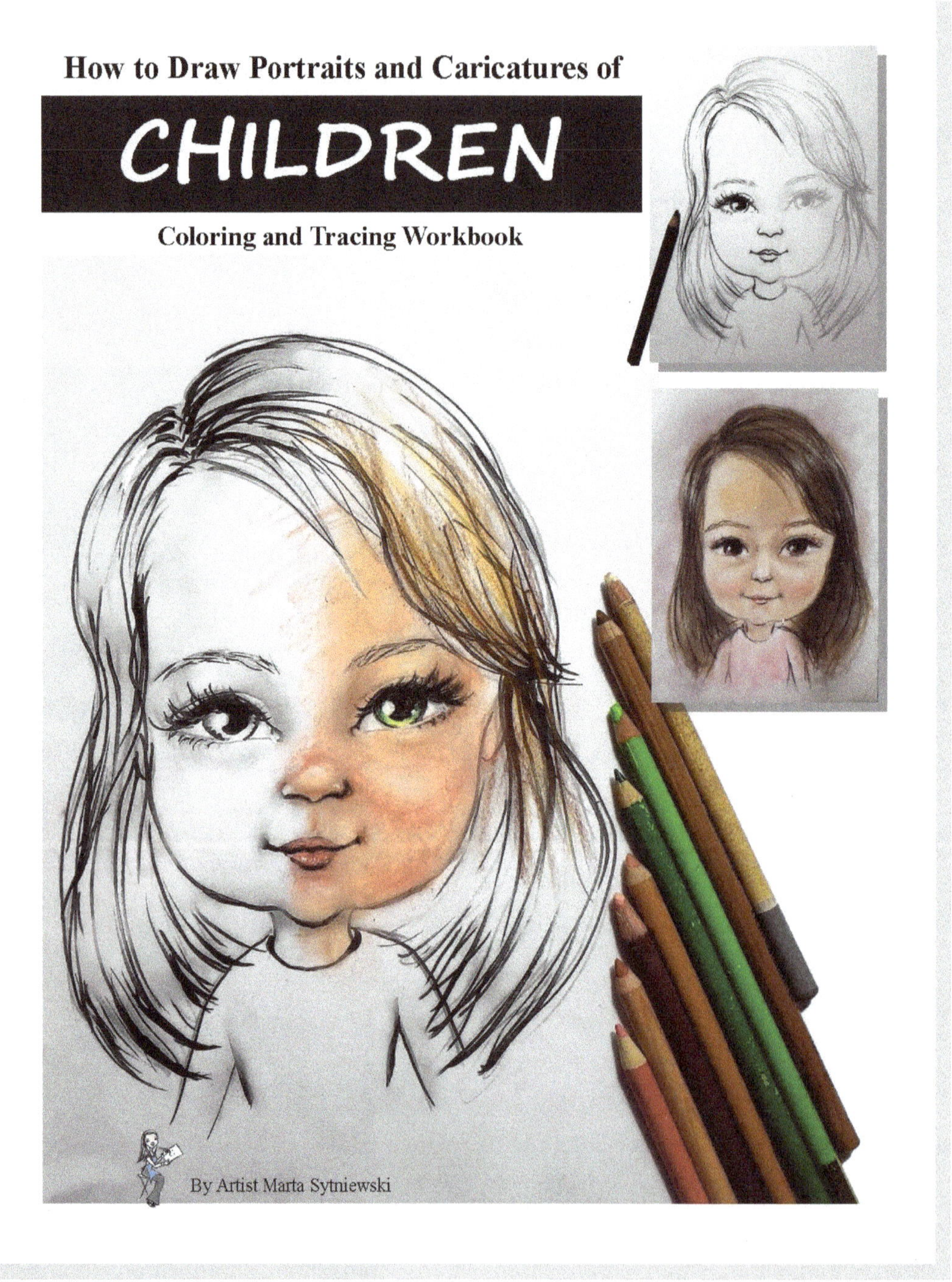